THE FIRST AMENDMENT
The Legacy of George Mason

GEORGE MASON

Painted in 1811 by D. W. Boudet, after a lost portrait by John Hesselius.

(Courtesy of the Virginia Museum, Richmond.)

THE GEORGE MASON LECTURES

THE FIRST AMENDMENT
The Legacy of George Mason

EDITED BY
T. DANIEL SHUMATE

FAIRFAX: *The George Mason University Press*
LONDON AND TORONTO: *Associated University Presses*

Associated University Presses
440 Forsgate Drive
Cranbury, New Jersey 08512

Associated University Presses
2133 Royal Windsor Drive, Unit 1
Mississauga, Ont., Canada L5J 1K5

Associated University Presses
25 Sicilian Avenue
London WC1A 2QH, England

The paper used in this publication meets the minimum requirements of the American National Standard for Permanence of Paper for Printed Library Materials Z39.48-1984.

Library of Congress Cataloging in Publication Data
Main entry under title:

The First Amendment.

Includes bibliographies and index.
1. Freedom of speech—United States. 2. Freedom of the press—United States. 3. Religious liberty—United States. 4. Mason, George, 1725–1792.
I. Shumate, T. Daniel
KF4770.F57 1985 342.73′0853 85-2958
ISBN 0-913969-05-2 347.302853

Printed in the United States of America

Contents

THE FIRST AMENDMENT
The Legacy of George Mason

Introduction

THE FIRST AMENDMENT TO THE CONSTITUTION IS "GEORGE MASON'S Legacy." Its fundamental elements—freedom of religion, and freedom of expression—were set forth in the Virginia Declaration of Rights in a form which profoundly influenced other state constitutions and the national Bill of Rights.

The long-neglected role of George Mason of Virginia in the political thought of the American revolutionary era, and in Western political thought generally, is increasingly regarded as both significant and complex by scholars responding to the approaching bicentennial of the Constitution. Understanding his thought and public activity in relation to the First Amendment guarantees an awareness of the evolution of English politics in these areas and the often conflicting concepts and practices which the early settlers brought to America; subsequent British developments and their influence on the American colonists; and in turn the evolution of the latter, conditioned by remoteness from the homeland and by looser economic and social environments, as they began diverging from the British models.

Mason and many other American leaders were influenced

in varying degrees by the Enlightenment, both English and Continental.[1] The 17th century in England had witnessed a phenomenal interest in the possibilities of human reason for understanding man and his world, both physical and social. The rationality discovered in "laws of nature" seemed equally applicable to human affairs to diminish the influence of "passion" and custom. Reasonable men welcomed John Locke's essays on government and toleration as a rationale for the Glorious Revolution of 1689, when a Stuart was overthrown peacefully and Parliamentary sovereignty asserted itself under a limited monarchy. The peaceful succession to the throne of the Protestant Hanoverians in 1714, following the demise of the last reigning Stuart, Queen Anne, was seen as reason put into practice.

Since England and the continent were the chief source of ideas and developments affecting the colonies, colonial gentlemen such as Mason's uncle John Mercer in nearby Stafford County built up extensive collections of English and European books, and Mercer's library was young George Mason's principal educational resource before he inaugurated his own at Gunston Hall. Mercer's collection included volumes on "natural philosophy," among them Newton's; on Continental thought concerning government and the law of nations; on the rise and fall of ancient republics and civilizations; and histories of the major contemporary nations of the European area (Russia, France, Turkey, and the Netherlands, among others).[2] With access to such collections, George Mason and other colonial leaders gained a larger perspective against which to judge events in their own lifetime and as a guide to action.

In the sphere of church-state relations Mason, by temperament an Anglican latitudinarian, drew much from the British Dissenter tradition, but preferred the more benign thought of

John Locke and natural rights philosophy. Religious dissent and reasonable political objectives had been important in the success of the Glorious Revolution and bore on the growing American claims to the full birthright of Englishmen. Such a viewpoint dictated religious tolerance, and although Mason's proclivities for social and political order favored prudence rather than libertarianism, he incorporated freedom of the press, and by implication speech, into his own catalogue of essential rights in the Virginia Declaration and in his advocacy of a federal bill of rights.

Ideas expressed in the national Bill of Rights, including the rights enumerated in the First Amendment, stemmed from the constitutional documents drafted by most of the newly proclaimed independent states, especially Virginia, and the American Declaration of Rights and the Appeal to the Inhabitants of Quebec, both issued in 1774 by the Continental Congress, prior to any of the revolutionary state constitutions. In the political and intellectual atmosphere of colonial America, the incipient revolutionary elements among the colonists sought to assert and justify their claims before public opinion. All these ideas were reiterated and developed in the constitutional ratification debates.

As drafted originally by George Mason, the Virginia Declaration of Rights was significantly strengthened by several committee additions, and liberalized in its article on religion. James Madison's proposal to substitute "free exercise of religion" for Mason's "Toleration" was accepted readily by Mason, whose original draft had apparently conformed to the English code.[3] The Virginia Declaration became the prototype of the bills of rights adopted by most of the other new states either as separate documents or embedded in the body of their constitutions, especially since it emanated from the largest and most populous of the new states—one already in the forefront of revolutionary political and military leadership, exemplified by Mason, Patrick Henry, and of course by George Washington.

When George Mason arrived in Williamsburg shortly after the Virginia Convention assembled in mid-May 1776 to act on the Continental Congress's advice to assume sovereign status, he was already recognized as a senior Virginia statesman, author of the Fairfax Resolves reacting to British closure of the Boston port, and of a widely-circulated letter during the earlier Stamp Act crisis. He was immediately asked to serve on the committee to draft a Declaration of Rights and a plan of government to replace royal authority. He drafted an initial list of 10 articles including Lockean principles of the purpose of government; this list was expanded in committee to 16 in the final version. Although the articles concerning freedom of the press and freedom of religion ranked near the end of the list, this was the first time in history that freedom of conscience and of the press was guaranteed by a Constitution.[4] Later when George Mason summarized the Virginia Declaration as the basis for Virginia's recommended amendments to the United States Constitution's First Amendment, he included freedom of speech along with freedom of the press and of conscience as essential bulwarks of liberty.

By 1780, eight of the other colonies (excepting Rhode Island and Connecticut, which were satisfied with their old charters) had adopted new constitutions with bills of rights or had embodied such rights in their constitutions. New Hampshire, after twice rejecting proposed constitutions for lack of a bill of rights, finally adopted a bill of rights in 1784, which enabled the constitution drawn up in 1780 to come into effect. Vermont, though not yet a state, nevertheless had a bill of rights.

In the new constitutions or bills of rights the prominence accorded the religious provision varied greatly, from second place (Pennsylvania and Delaware) and third (Massachusetts) to 33rd (Maryland). Position in a listing, however, was no indication of its importance. Virginia, for example, which ranked religious freedom last in its Declaration of Rights, soon began to dismantle the establishment and finally joined Rhode Island in according full legal scope for religious freedom. Some degree of establishment, usually in the provision for public tax support of a particular church unless otherwise designated, still existed in Massachusetts, Connecticut, New Hampshire, Maryland and South Carolina. Adherence to "Christianity" was a condition for enjoying religious liberty in two states, and it was made clear that this must be the Protestant variety in six other states. Even liberal Pennsylvania required affirmation of belief in the divine inspiration of the Bible and in a future state of rewards and punishments for office holders.[5]

Bills of rights sometimes provided more liberal affirmations than constitutions. Thus, New York, which granted free exercise of religious preference and worship, in its requirements for naturalization effectively barred Catholics by requiring renunciation of any allegiance to foreign powers and potentates, both ecclesiastical and civil.[6] Nevertheless, the very existence of guarantees of religious freedom in most of the states provided powerful reinforcement for Madison's later efforts to have Congress adopt the first amendment.

The scope of free expression was enlarged to include speech in 1776 when Pennsylvania provided in its Declaration of Rights that "the people have a right to freedom of speech, and of writing, and publishing their sentiments . . ." "Therefore the freedom of the press ought not to be restricted." This was an epoch-making constitutional guarantee of free speech, the first in history. Vermont in 1777, even though not officially a state until 1791, was the only state to follow Pennsylvania's lead. Delaware, Georgia, Massachusetts, New Hampshire,

North and South Carolina also provided for freedom of the press; thus seven of the original 13 states felt that liberty of the press was essential.[7]

These declarations become even more meaningful in light of earlier Colonial history. After all, settlers of most of the states enforced religious conformity—Anglicanism in the southern colonies, Congregationalism in most of New England. This conformity is inseparable from the traditional concept of church-state relations in Britain during the 17th and 18th centuries. Similarly, the relationship of the press to government in the English development of the concept and practice of freedom of expression must be noted before developments in America can be understood. Since freedom of the press and freedom of speech were seldom clearly distinguished until the late 18th century, this discussion will focus primarily on the press as the medium of expression. Freedom of assembly and petition, added to the First Amendment only in the final congressional debates, will be noted only incidentally.

Religious Toleration in England

The long-standing conflict between church and crown in England came to a head with Henry VIII's seizure of control of the English Church. The emphasis of Henry VIII and his Tudor and Stuart successors on conformity—or as the statutes put it, "uniformity"—stemmed from reasons of state: the preservation of the throne precariously won in the late 15th century after the Lancaster-York rivalries ended, Roman Catholic efforts to restore England to Catholicism, and radical Protestant unhappiness after Henry nationalized the English Church but made no basic reform in doctrine or "popish" organization and liturgical practices.

Henry was able to exploit a rising tide of secular as well as religiously motivated interests in curbing the influence of the Catholic Church in all spheres of English life—political and economic as well as religious.[8] He viewed repression and persecution primarily as means of achieving political, not religious ends. Henry's immediate successors, Edward VI and Mary, sought to tilt the scales toward, respectively, the Protestant and Catholic side, and the latter precipitated sharp internal divisions which threatened the fabric of the nation.

Their brief reigns gave way to a true Henrician in the person of Elizabeth.[9] The institutional arrangements known as the Elizabethan Compromise built on and consolidated Henry's foundation for the political and religious life of England and persisted as an ideal throughout the century in which most of the American colonies were founded. Under terms of the Settlement, Elizabeth was Supreme Governor of the Church and acted through Parliament to prescribe the articles of doctrine, the organization and the liturgy of the national church. All English subjects were considered members of the Church of England and bound to it by the Act of Uniformity, which required at least outward conformity to its doctrines and liturgy set forth in the *Book of Common Prayer.* Elizabeth established an Ecclesiastical Court of High Commission to assist the royal policing of ecclesiastical matters, and the dreaded Star Chamber, with its cloak of secrecy and power over political disaffection, was branching off from the royal Council as a high court. While her policies in retrospect seemed to some a model of good sense and comprehensiveness, they nevertheless antagonized the reformist Puritan wing of the Church and, of course, Catholics. Anti-Catholicism was notably enflamed, especially among the Puritans, by the Spanish onslaught and the Armada.

The accession in 1603 of the first Stuart, James I, was at first welcomed by all parties. But his and his successors' problems in handling English political and religious affairs lay in their attempts to obtain precise definitions of the limits of their power, which they insisted was absolute by divine right. Thus at the Hampton Court conference of 1604 James uttered his memorable threat: ". . . I shall make them conforme themselves, or I will harrie them out of the land, or else do worse." This public humiliation of the still moderate Puritans was compounded by his declaration to Parliament that he could not tolerate Puritans but had no desire to persecute, and by his reference to the loyalty of many Catholic laity despite priests who took seriously the papal claim of the power to dethrone heretical kings.

By Charles's accession in 1625 the Anglican and Puritan factions were sharply and visibly at odds. Some Separatist Puritans had fled to more tolerant Calvinist Holland, whence a handful of "Pilgrims" came to America in 1621, and the stream of Puritan refugees to New England began in earnest when Charles I's principal adviser, Archbishop William Laud, implemented the policy of "harrying out of the land" those who refused to conform in every particular to High Church practice.

While many Puritans in mid-century became Presbyterians, many others became Independents, the label for a variety of Calvinist sects who were much more loosely organized than Presbyterians, and known variously as Brownists, Separatists, and Congregationalists. The Pilgrim Fathers stem from the Separatist category. Baptists, though dating from the 16th century on the Continent, had been vigorously suppressed in England under the Tudors, but were finally gaining a firm foothold in England in the 1620's. Soon, however, Calvinist schismatics from the Congregationalists organized a Baptist sect later important in the colonies, the "Particular" Baptists, which competed with the theologically more liberal earlier groups.

Lay thinkers, including some clergy who began to consider religion and church-state relations more in a secular than a religious context, were to be found in England early in the 17th century. With an influence far exceeding their small numbers, they slowly impacted the political-religious situation in England. The more religious-minded are often described as Latitudinarians, moderates despairing equally of extreme Anglican intolerance and Puritan fanaticism, who turned to reason and moderation to settle theological turmoil.

Morality was far more important than doctrine to the Latitudinarians, and for the broad, though less numerous, category comprised of Rationalists and Skeptics. Both Latitudinarians and Rationalists/Skeptics were attracted by the liberal and humanist Arminian movement in Dutch Calvinism, revolting against extreme predestinarian Calvinism. Dutch Arminians included Hugo Grotius, famous as an expounder of the natural law whose ideas attracted followers in England and the colonies as well as on the continent. Religious rationalists, admiring the seeming perfection of nature as revealed by science, became deists and remained nominally within the Church.

Charles I's political and religious intransigeance, reflected by a decade of personal rule without summoning Parliament, had united members of Parliament against him regardless of their religious views and forced him to summon the Long Parliament in 1640. Parliament divided almost evenly, however, over the Grand Remonstrance of 1641, which called for sweeping reform in state and church. During the Civil War of the 1640's Parliament negotiated for Scottish military support; the price was a promise to establish Presbyterianism as the national church in England. The parliamentary army also was under the sway of Calvinists—mostly Independents, Baptists and other sectarians, and the Independent general Oliver Cromwell was rapidly becoming its foremost commander and spokesman. It was the army which, once Charles was defeated, forced a rump Parliament to try and then execute Charles in 1649.

The Presbyterians dreamed of a godly state and church modeled on Calvin's Geneva, to be achieved by repressing all disagreement if necessary. The Anglican Church was completely disestablished, the episcopacy abolished, and many Anglican clergy ousted from parishes for religious or political disaffection. Parliament, now with real power in the absence of the monarchy, set about prescribing the organization, discipline and worship for a reformed national church and, though with political misgivings, tried to accommodate the Presbyterian clergy's extremist wishes.

Widespread dissatisfaction with the Presbyterians grew within the army; Cromwell and the Independents in the army and in Parliament seized control and finally set up the Protectorate in 1655 to stabilize the realm. Lord Protector Cromwell was more tolerant, except toward Catholic Ireland, than most of his followers and attempted to institutionalize religious tolerance for all except Catholics, Anglicans who refused to relinquish episcopacy and the Prayer Book, non-Trinitarians, and atheists. In practice he tried to administer the laws passed by Parliament leniently, and even urged the readmission to England of Jews, excluded since the Middle Ages.

When Cromwell died in 1658 his son Richard lacked both the talent and skill necessary to prolong the Protectorate, and the great majority of English, still fundamentally Anglican and wearied by two decades of political, religious and military strife, were ready for restoration of the monarchy as a symbol of stability. In 1660 new elections were called and the resulting Parliament rapidly voted to reestablish royal government in cooperation with Parliament. Nevertheless the interregnum period had been fruitful in thinking concerning the nature of church and state and their relationship.

Once Charles II returned from exile and was proclaimed

king, the Church of England was reestablished and its bishops recovered their place in the restored House of Lords, though the Lords' political power was now considerably weakened.[10] Charles II was inclined to be tolerant of dissenters, as his immediate grant of a charter for Rhode Island indicates, and thanks to the Catholic support he had received in exile was especially sympathetic to the plight of English Catholics during the Puritan hegemony. Members of the Cavalier Parliament elected after his call to power were overwhelmingly Anglican and resentful of their own and their church's treatment during the Interregnum. This anger found expression in the "Clarendon Code," a series of laws aimed at Protestant dissenters, Catholics and miscellaneous heretics, severely penalizing all who refused to attend divine services or who attended dissenting conventicles. A new Act of Uniformity reauthorized the Prayer Book and articles of belief, and the Corporation Act excluded from participation in municipal government all who refused the sacrament according to Anglican rites. All nonconforming clergy were ousted from their parishes.

By now Protestant dissenters had dwindled to about one-twentieth of the population and Catholics even less. Charles's two efforts to issue Declarations of Indulgence superseding all penal laws against both Protestants and Catholics were blocked by fear of internal "popery" and Catholic France, as well as by suspicion of the royal motives. In 1672 Parliament emphasized this stance by passing the Test Act, requiring every officeholder, civil or military, to take the sacrament according to Anglican usage, to swear oaths of supremacy and allegiance, and to make a declaration against the Catholic doctrine of transubstantiation.

James II precipitated new crises in announcing his intention to set aside the Test Act—in reality so Catholics could serve as officers in his standing army. In 1688 he issued a Declaration of Indulgence suspending the penal laws against

Catholics and Dissenters and required that the Anglican clergy read the Indulgence text from the pulpit. When the Archbishop of Canterbury and six bishops petitioned the king to withdraw his order and criticized the royal dispensing power, James charged them with seditious libel. This "Case of the Seven Bishops" was to help shape Article 5 in the English Bill of Rights, concerning the right of subjects to petition the king without commitment to prison or a charge of seditious libel unless requested by two judges.[11]

In these circumstances, James's opponents invited William of Orange and his Stuart wife Mary to take the throne. An experienced publicist, William saw the value of showing moderation in printed tracts designed for the general public as well as the upper class.

The draft Declaration of Rights prepared for William's signature, the basis for the Bill of Rights of 1689, contained 13 articles chosen by a House of Commons committee. They dealt with three general questions: royal power with respect to the law, royal military power with respect to a standing army in peacetime, and royal power of toleration. Concerning religion, the Declaration declared the royal dispensing power illegal and the Toleration Act of 1689 ended permanently the idea of an inclusive state church in England. The act allowed Trinitarians willing to submit to most of the 39 Articles of Religion to preach and teach freely provided they obtained licenses. Although the licensing requirement was less vigorously enforced as the 18th century wore on, licensing ended only in 1779.[12]

After the Glorious Revolution the Church's position steadily weakened, in part because of the spreading influence of Enlightenment thinking. The philosopher of the Glorious Revolution and its sequel was John Locke, whose theme was "Reason must be our judge and guide in everything." Locke argued that "the whole jurisdiction of the magistrate reaches only to civil concernments . . . it neither can nor ought in any manner to be extended to the salvation of souls." Religious truth could defend itself; there was no need for secret dissenter conventicles. "If solemn assemblies . . . be permitted to any one sort of professors, all these things ought to be permitted for the Presbyterians, Independents, Anabaptists, Arminians, Quakers and others . . ." Even Jews, Mohammedans and pagans should have civil rights. He would exclude only those with opinions he regarded as harmful to the community, those believing faith should not be kept with heretics, those serving or seeking protection of a foreign prince, and those denying the existence of God.[13]

Though Locke himself was Anglican, his views on toleration appealed to many dissenters, who now preferred to fight politically for their rights as Englishmen, not as reformed religionists.

The intellectual reaction to this state of affairs was centered in the "Real Whigs" or "Commonwealthmen" harking back to and broadening the views on religious and political toleration of John Milton, James Harrington and Algernon Sidney among others. Several generations of Commonwealthmen reiterated the need for toleration through tracts, sermons and books and liberalized the attitude of some Anglicans as well as dissenters. Benjamin Franklin and other Americans in England and also many at home were influenced and encouraged by Commonwealthmen. So far as Real Whigs were concerned, political and religious liberty were inseparable, and their arguments helped the colonists come to the same conclusion.[14]

Speech and Press in England

Medieval statutes for suppressing rumors concerning king and nobility as well as the Catholic Church's desire to suppress any manifestation of heresy form the background for the long contest between government and freedom of speech and press in English history. Tudor England was the seedbed for the Stuart and Cromwellian systems aimed at controlling public inquiry and discussion concerning foreign and domestic affairs. Magna Carta and other feudal limitations on the royal power were disregarded by Henry VIII as he manipulated discontent with Catholicism to advance his political interests.[15]

Public interest in religion and in political affairs was stimulated by the spread of printing in the vernacular tongue and by the overtly political as well as religious character of the English Reformation. A royal proclamation added "seditious opinions" as well as heresy and theological error as grounds for government action, and set up a licensing system for all books printed in England, with penalties of loss of all goods and chattels and imprisonment at the will of the crown. The reigns of Edward VI and Mary each began with leniency and concluded with strict controls over printing and attempts to catch "talebearers" and rumor spreaders among the quarreling factions.

Elizabeth, as Supreme Governor of the Church, issued royal injunctions in 1559 providing that all new works must apply for approval to the queen, Privy Council or an ecclesiastical official, and that names of the licensed printers must appear at the end of each work. This constituted the basis for all subsequent licensing in England and the colonies. The Stationers Company, the corporation of printers and stationers, became administrator of the royal registers of publications.

Rumblings of revolt came from a few defiant printers, religious nonconformists (mostly Puritans returned from exile) and a few bold members of Parliament. Puritan writings increased to the point that Elizabeth employed a Star Chamber decree in 1586 to try to tighten the licensing system. The

Puritans, however, were interested in enforcing the printing regulations against others rather than in general freedom. They used the press to appeal to the nation. When some Puritans attacked the Anglican Church in a tract in 1572, after their arrest they argued they had acted while Parliament was in session, and this linked the ancient right to petition with freedom of the press. Peter Wentworth, a member of Parliament, objected to suppression of the right to introduce bills concerning religion and the royal succession, and this planted the germ of the idea of "liberty of speech" for members of Parliament. Its significance has been compared by one historian to Luther's posting of his theses at Wittenberg.[16]

The early Stuarts found themselves frequently on the defensive as restless Parliaments sought to expand their own rights to free speech against royal and clerical opposition. Simultaneously they tried to control if not suppress any public discussion of what they regarded as properly parliamentary affairs.

James I at first sought public support by publishing books expounding his policies, but soon his Star Chamber Court took the unprecedented step of ignoring a key restriction of the medieval statutes governing suppression of "any false News or Tales"—the stipulation that the matter reported was in fact false. Thus prosecution was facilitated, since truth was no longer a defense, and publication by writing or printing, as well as "invention" of the item in question, became sufficient basis for prosecution. Furthermore, the scope of the ecclesiastical Court of High Commission in controlling printed matter was broadened. With English interest in the Thirty Years War, public hunger for information rather than argument was growing near the close of James' reign, but only the wealthy could afford the few newsletters. Dutch printers supplied English desires for news sheets, and English printers soon followed suit, ignoring royal prohibitions.

During the 1620's a monopoly for printing censored foreign newsletters was granted but for a time news sheets, ballads and almanacs could be published without licensing. Charles I's Privy Council ordered the suppression of all newsbooks, and booksellers became equally liable to prosecution. Public interest in the tense domestic political and religious situation arising from Archbishop Laud's policies was heightened by the king's highhanded treatment of Parliament. In 1637, a Star Chamber decree set up detailed regulations for licensing all books and pamphlets, including their title, introduction, and dedication. Evasions were checked by requiring names of the author, printer, and licenser to be printed and requiring new licenses for all reprints.

During the Puritan Revolution press regulation was confused after the Star Chamber and the Court of High Commission were abolished and the Stationers Company's authority was weakened as its members shifted allegiance from crown to Parliament. Parliament especially wished to control printing of or about its proceedings, but for several years hundreds of new publications of parliamentary proceedings appeared. The desire of Parliament and other political groups to appear in a favorable public light and individuals' fear for their souls if the government interfered with the printing of religious truths contributed to the new interest in domestic news.

The Army threat to Parliament after the Self-Denying Ordinance had severely weakened that body led in 1647 to the most stringent printing ordinance thus far. There were vigorous efforts to suppress news of and comment on the execution of the king in 1649. The Parliament and General Fairfax had issued orders constituting warrants to search for and seize all unlicensed printers, and the Treason Act of 1649 provided that any person writing against the government or the Army was guilty of treason and liable to execution. The printing act of 1647 was continued till Cromwell as Lord Protector established his own controls, after which all printed news sheets except one favored by the government were rapidly suppressed.

Of the numerous advocates of free expression during the Interregnum a few are still invoked. John Lilburne, a radical pamphleteer persecuted for seditious tracts by the Star Chamber, demanded freedom of the press as a freeborn Englishman and challenged the then dominant Presbyterians to public debate: "For if you had not been men that had been afraid of your cause, you would have been willing to have fought and contended with us upon even grounds and equal terms, namely that the Presse might be open for us as you." This was published in 1647 without license or the required imprint. Ironically Presbyterian members of Parliament who themselves had suffered persecution earlier were now zealous to suppress non-approved public discussion. In the absence of other means of expressing opposition to a bigoted Parliament, the politically and socially radical Leveller party was born. Its principles included a written constitution, limited powers, separation of powers, and freedom of the press—ideas advocated later by George Mason. The Leveller petition of January 18, 1649 eloquently urged revocation of all ordinances blocking free publication:

> As for any prejudice to Government thereby, if Government be just in its constitution, and equal in its distributions, it will be good, if not absolutely necessary for them, to hear all voices and judgements, which they can never do, but by giving freedom to the Press, and in case any abuse their authority by scandalous pamphlets, they will never want Advocates to vindicate their innocency. And therefore all things being duly weighed, to refer all Books and Pamphlets to the judgement, discretion or affection of Licensers, or to put the least restraint upon the Press, seems . . . expressly opposite and dangerous to the liberties of the

> people, and to be carefully avoided, as any other exorbitancy or prejudice in Government.[17]

Parliament retaliated by passing the Treason Act and tried Lilburne under it. The jury refused to convict.

John Milton's interest in the freedom of the press arose from difficulties with the Stationers Company and government officials over his pamphlets on divorce. Editions of his first tract in 1643 and 1644 were unlicensed. The Stationers Company, two of whose wardens had licensed another edition, averted Parliament's wrath by discovering that the unlicensed tracts contained opinions objectionable to the Company and haled Milton before their Committee on Printing. This occasioned Milton's renowned *Areopagitica: A Speech of Mr. John Milton For the Liberty of Unlicensed Printing to the Parliament of England,* printed without license. In the *Areopagitica* Milton attacked the licensing principle but focused primarily on intellectual liberty for the responsible and serious minded who might hold differing opinions. He had no brief for Catholics or for journalists. Though famous today, Milton's *Areopagitica* was apparently ignored until republished in the 1730's when English interest in the Zenger case in New York was at its peak.

At the Restoration, all Puritan acts and decrees affecting printing were voided except the abolition of the Star Chamber, to which Charles I had belatedly agreed. By now Parliament had finally established its jurisdiction over control of printing but the King did not give up the prerogative of suppressing and licensing and invited Parliament to assist in press regulation. The Printing Act of 1662 was passed and renewed (with one brief lapse) until its expiration in 1694, after which licensing was no longer required in theory. In practice, it continued to be into the 18th century, as the American colonists discovered.

The Act of 1662 limited printing to members of the Stationers Company and printers of the two universities, and also limited the number of presses and apprentices per master printer. Booksellers were to be members of the Stationers Company or persons specially licensed by the bishop of the vendor's diocese. Nothing could be printed, imported or sold if "heretical, seditious, schismatical or offensive" to the Christian faith or the Church of England, or offensive to any government official, corporation or private person. A Surveyor of the Press, Roger L'Estrange, operated under the principal secretaries of state from 1662 to 1679, and handled all licensing of "books of history and affairs of state." Under ecclesiastical licensing authority works on divinity, philosophy "and anything else" were the responsibility of the Archbishop of Canterbury and the Bishop of London, yet in practice L'Estrange handled much of this also.[18]

The secretaries of state were empowered to issue general and special warrants for searches and seizures, even though general warrants were illegal for other felonies. A general warrant issued to L'Estrange permitted him to "seize all seditious books and libels and to apprehend the authors, contrivers, printers, publishers, and dispersers of them, and bring them before him to be proceeded against according to law" and to "search any house, shop printing room, chamber, warehouse, etc., for seditious, scandalous or unlicensed pictures, books or papers, to bring away or deface the same, and the letter press, taking away all the copies and to search for and proceed against all printers, authors, publishers, or dispersers of the same." Printers and booksellers could be jailed under the secretaries' judicial authority. The use of such warrants against the press was unchallenged until the notorious John Wilkes case under George III.

A government newspaper, the *London Gazette,* was established during the Great Plague, its contents mostly official announcements concerning internal affairs or official reports of foreign affairs. It was quickly recognized as an instrument of whichever ministry was in power and its circulation dwindled while independent papers flourished. Nevertheless, it set a precedent for many future colonial newspapers titled *Gazette* including those in Virginia and Maryland. Many of these had a close relationship to the colonial administrations as purveyors of the official view.

The Glorious Revolution of 1688–1689 occurred at a time when the size of the electorate had grown considerably (to more than 200,000) and the national increase in literacy, including many "middling" and marginal folk in the socioeconomic scale, had reinforced the desire to use printed communications. James II vigorously enforced censorship and issued orders to compel all coffeehouses to permit only the official *Gazette* on their premises. A royal proclamation in late 1688 forbade discussion of political affairs "by writing, printing, speaking or listening"![19]

There is no mention of freedom of speech and press in the Declaration of Rights produced by the Glorious Revolution but the more relaxed attitude of government was indicated when the Printing Act was allowed to expire in 1694. This was in large part a result of recognition of fundamental changes in the political system. The Tory and Whig factions were becoming more distinct, and party newspapers had begun to appear late in the reign of Charles II. Although the Lords wished to revive the controls, the Commons opposed on the grounds of its likely effect on the "commerce" of the printing industry. The argument for commerce has been attributed to John Locke and to a new awareness that attempts to suppress sedition via licensing acts were ineffective and damaging to the printing trade. Sporadic efforts to revive the act continued until the end of Anne's reign. While none of this altered the prohibition on non-official reporting of proceedings of Parliament, the Commons had permitted official publication of its votes on major issues since 1680.

Queen Anne, her ministers and the Anglican clergy were aghast at the flood of pamphlets and papers discussing grave matters of state and church, and the Queen issued one futile prohibition after another. Toward the end of her reign a happy solution seemed to arise out of the government's vigorous search for new revenues to finance the prolonged wars against Louis XIV. A tax on printed matter would not only provide revenue but have the further advantage of forcing ephemeral publications, especially newspapers, to shut down for economic reasons. Books, defined as publications containing more than six octavo pages, were exempt. All papers and pamphlets printed in London, which meant the bulk of them, must be registered at the Stamp Office and bear the name and address of the publisher or face a heavy fine. Newspaper advertisements were also taxed.

Many newspapers expired, hit by rising production costs and a decline in higher priced subscriptions, but in a very short time publishers realized that the wording of the Stamp Act left convenient loopholes, and after the accession of George I compliance was minimal.

This was the first stamp tax on the press tried in the 18th century. A second under Walpole also languished until the elder Pitt in 1757 increased the tax on newspapers and advertising to help finance the Seven Years War. These were the precedents for Charles Townshend's unfortunate plan to oblige the American colonists also to share the financial burden of the midcentury wars by levying a stamp tax on documents and other printed matter in the colonies.

In the face of difficulties for newspapers in the early 18th century, the anonymous pamphlet became the chief political weapon until regular papers were placed on a sounder economic footing by party or official subsidies. Literary figures with moderate views, such as Addison, Steele, and Swift, who had played prominent roles in later Stuart journalism, began to give way to political journalists, typified by Thomas Gordon and John Trenchard. Collaborating from 1720 to 1722 in the pseudonymous *Letters of Cato,* they became celebrated for their sharp running criticism of the government's political, economic and religious controls. "Cato's" influence extended to the American colonies, and the name was invoked frequently as colonial restiveness with royal control mounted.

The apogee of the doctrine of seditious libel was reached with a formal definition by Chief Justice Holt in 1704 that it comprised anything tending to lessen public affection for the government.[20] The doctrine encountered new problems in the 18th century when, in both England and the colonies, juries rebelled at the restrictions it placed on their historic function of pronouncing verdicts of guilt or innocence. The phrase "freedom of the press" began to appear in the courts in the 1730's and was used in the House of Commons after the widespread interest aroused by publication in London of proceedings in the Zenger trial in New York discussed below.

The desultory public debate on the question of freedom of speech and press conducted since the "Cato" letters, came to a head with the celebrated affair of John Wilkes in the 1760's as part of the running fight between Whigs and George III's Tory ministers. In the famous No. 45 of the *North Briton,* Wilkes was regarded as having insulted the king himself by declaring that a speech from the throne, prepared and delivered by one of George III's ministers, was deplorably in error. A general warrant led to the arrest of Wilkes, his printer and publisher and many others and in seizure of his personal papers. He fled to France after conviction both for seditious libel and for criminal libel, the latter on the basis of an unpublished manuscript procured by the government. Outlawed when he failed to appear for sentencing, he returned after letters and tracts he wrote in Paris had aroused public support, and went to jail only on the criminal libel count. Aside from the sensational political maneuvers he undertook concerning the legality of his election to Parliament, Wilkes' importance for free speech and a free press lies in his concern with the issues of the general warrant and search and seizure. General warrants, even in cases of seditious libel, were finally pronounced invalid by Chief Justice Lord Mansfield in 1765. This aspect of the Wilkes affair had far reaching implications for liberty in general and freedom of press and speech in particular in America as well as England.[21]

One of the important contributors to the debate on free expression was William Bollen, an American, former advocate general for Massachusetts Bay and former resident agent in England for the colony, who had published in 1766 *Freedom of Speech and Writing Upon Public Affairs, Considered, with an Historical Review.* He was one of the first to distinguish freedom of speech and freedom of the press in his writing. However, Bollen did not criticize the wisdom of continued abuses of seditious libel despite its shaky foundation.[22] One authority on English press and speech freedom in the period characterizes Bollen's work as thus far "surely the most learned work in English on the subject of free speech, and along with that of James Alexander, the only other important contribution by an American in the 18th century."

To this point the question of the legal basis for seditious libel had not been seriously challenged. Nearly all commentators had suggested that some means of restraining untrue, malicious and false attacks on government was essential. The real challenge came in the public debate stirred up by the Wilkes affair. An anonymous legal authority using the pen name "Father of Candor," replying to a tract defending the government's treatment of Wilkes, proved that seditious libel dated historically only from Elizabeth's Star Chamber and asserted that the Glorious Revolution would have been impossible without numerous violations of the doctrine of seditious libel. The liberty of "exposing and opposing bad administration" was a necessary right of a free people. Using the same tactics earlier publicized in the Zenger trial, "Father of Candor" declared that jurors, not judges, should decide whether an accused's words were libellous, since most prosecutions for seditious libel were really quarrels between government and the people. Libels were generally held to be criminal because of their tendency to breach the peace, but words were not criminal *per se*. The author came close to advocating the concept of the overt act as a test of criminality in such cases. Very few before him had even hinted at this with reference to free expression. This principle remained a goal for future development in England and America.[23]

One of the published letters of a series signed "Junius" in 1769–70 went beyond Wilkes's attack on the king by accusing George III directly as the fount of evils in the administration. No longer able to control the verdict of juries in seditious libel cases, the Attorney General resorted first to charging the vendor, who was convicted on the basis of Lord Mansfield's charge to the jury as guilty of "publication by sale." The publishers, however, were found not guilty. In the course of heated public discussion of the trial Lord Mansfield called a special session of the House of Lords to explain his views. Lord Camden seized the opportunity to pose questions to the Chief Justice concerning the scope of the jury's role in seditious libel cases, and challenged the right of judges to determine the criminality of publication while leaving only the determination of the fact of publication to the jury. Under political pressure from the crown as well as those agreeing with Lord Camden, Mansfield promised a reply but failed to deliver it for more than a decade. Only Fox's Libel Act of 1792 finally settled the matter, much too late to affect American constitutional law in its formative period.[24]

Religion in the Colonies

The religious liberty guaranteed in the First Amendment to the Constitution was the product of slow evolution, varying from colony to colony. Its development depended partly on the time and circumstances in England accompanying the foundation of particular colonies, and partly on the new environment facing transplanted Europeans far from English political and ecclesiastical control. As the religious circumstances of England changed, the colonies both reflected events in England and resisted or raced ahead of them as the internal colonial pressures dictated.[25]

Each of the major religious trends in England found a secure niche in at least one, sometimes several, of the American colonies at the moment of their foundation. Anglicanism was firmly established in Virginia, founded at a time (1607) when the first Stuart king of England began asserting claims of the state church against the troublesome and growing Puritan wing of that church. By the end of the century, the establishment of the Anglican Church had occurred unevenly in the other southern colonies and in a small but significant area of New York as a result of the conquest of New Netherland. Puritans were in absolute control from the beginning in all New England except Rhode Island, where Roger Williams and the Baptists predominated. Quakers controlled early Pennsylvania and West Jersey; and Catholics were for a time provided a haven from any persecution in Maryland. Presbyterianism found little reception anywhere until the Scotch-Irish streamed into Pennsylvania and made it a stronghold and radiating center of Presbyterian influence. As time passed, each of these groups except the Catholics found major opportunities for expansion in other colonies.

Catholicism suffered in the English colonies as well as in England from its feared and hated association with Spain and France, both competitors with England in North America—Spain for the entire colonial period, France until driven out by the British conquest of New France in the early 1760's. Jews were generally no more welcome in America than in England, though Parliament granted the possibility of naturalization in the colonies in 1740.

The little Plymouth Colony represented the then precarious Separatist tradition of the early 17th century in England rather than mainstream Puritanism, which accounts for the flight of the "Pilgrims" to the Netherlands before departing in 1620, with others from England, for the New World. Plymouth remained a small, weak colony with its own Calvinist established church until absorbed into Massachusetts Bay late in the century.

Massachusetts Bay as finally chartered in 1629 was nominally a trading company with Puritan mercantile backing and Puritans predominant in its affairs. The Puritan leadership, under John Winthrop, maneuvered to transfer the Company together with its charter to New England, where an advance party had already settled at Salem and set up a covenanted church and government under John Endicott. This model was continued but unlike the Pilgrims, these Puritans originally had no intention of breaking completely with the Church of England, a feature sharply criticized by Roger Williams, an avowed Separatist, when he arrived in 1631. As the tide of Puritan migration to New England proceeded in the 1630's and the homeland moved toward civil strife between Puritans and the monarchy, the church of Massachusetts Bay elaborated what became the New England Congregational establishment, consisting of independent congregations loosely affiliated but all held firmly within the Calvinist doctrinal framework. The influence of the clergy on the state was exercised not directly but through its role in determining church membership and conduct and the high regard in which it was held. The state supported the churches by public taxation and the enforcement of its discipline by godly magistrates, elected by a franchise confined to church members. Massachusetts treated all dissenters—Anglicans, Baptists, Quakers, Catholics—very harshly until the stubborn colony's charter was revoked and replaced by royal government near the end of the 17th century. Then Anglican worship was introduced by armed force and the Toleration Act of 1689 began to be felt.

The principal offshoot of Massachusetts was Puritan Connecticut, the union of independent settlements on the Connecticut River and around New Haven which were similar to Massachusetts in church and state relationships and practices. Puritans were predominant also in New Hampshire and East Jersey, and for a time gained a preponderant position in Maryland.

Puritans regarded Rhode Island, whose chief founder was Roger Williams, as the black spot of New England because of his radically tolerant policies. Williams succeeded in uniting Providence with several other settlements under a charter for Rhode Island and Providence Plantations during the Puritan interregnum in England. Fearing that this charter might be invalidated at the Restoration, he persuaded Charles II to issue another containing the often-quoted statement: ". . . it is much in their hearts . . . to hold forth a livelie experiment, that a most flourishing civil state may stand and best be maintained . . . with a full libertie in religious concernements . . . ." Assuming that distance would prevent disturbance to uniformity in England, the royal will desired "that no person within the sayd colonie . . . shall bee any wise molested, punished, disquieted or called in question, for any differences in opinione in matters of religion, and doe not actually disturb the civill peace of our royal colony . . . ." This was the first embodiment of religious liberty in fundamental law.[26]

This provision was copied in the first charter of Carolina in 1665 and, with different wording, in another of 1669. It appears almost verbatim in two documents issued by colonial proprietors: the Concessions of Proprietors of Carolina of 1665, and the Concession of New Jersey in 1664.[27] That these colonies copied the Rhode Island statement, however, did not imply that they implemented it. For example, the Anglican Church was established firmly in Carolina, first in South Carolina and later in North Carolina, where it remained weak but nevertheless legally privileged.

A parallel but for the colonies perhaps more important source of the idea of legal toleration appeared with the influence of William Penn, first as one of several Quakers who purchased the proprietorship of West Jersey, later as sole proprietor of Pennsylvania. Penn drafted constitutional documents for both areas. In his first Frame of Government of Pennsylvania in 1662 he appended a section on "Laws Agreed Upon in England" in which religious liberty was specified, though other articles required Sabbath observance and punished immorality, including blasphemy. After the Glorious Revolution Penn lost his proprietorship because of his close ties with the Stuarts, but it was soon restored. His reissue of the Frame of Government, after repeating the guarantee of religious liberty, added a restriction on officeholding to believers in Jesus Christ.

Historically Catholic Maryland ranks first in terms of a toleration act in the colonies, the Act Concerning Religion in 1649. The second Lord Baltimore, whose father had converted from Anglicanism but continued in favor under James I, was granted a proprietary charter in 1632 by

Charles I as a haven for Catholics. The charter itself contained no reference to religious toleration, but it instructed the governors to avoid any offense to Protestants. The first settlers in 1634 were a few Catholic gentlemen and a much larger predominantly Protestant body of servants and laborers. Few Catholics cared to leave England under the second Stuart king during the first decade of the colony. However, Puritans were growing in number and, encouraged by the rising Puritan power in England, threatened the colonial government. To calm the situation, the proprietor appointed a Protestant governor and in 1649 seems to have prodded the Catholics in the Assembly to join Protestants in ratifying what became known as the Toleration Act. Its conclusion reads:

> . . . noe person or persons whatsoever within this Province . . . professing to believe in Jesus Christ, shall from henceforth bee any waies troubled, molested or discountenanced for or in respect of his or her religion nor in the free exercise thereof . . . nor any way compelled to the beleife or exercise of any other Religion against his or her consent. . . .[28]

These liberal provisions were hedged in by other articles providing the death penalty for denying the Trinity; and forbidding denigration of the Virgin, Apostles and Evangelists and the use of derogatory appellations such as "papist" or "puritan" for other religious groups.

When a Catholic Royalist succeeded the Protestant governor in 1651, the Puritan Parliament of England sent a commission which asserted parliamentary authority and temporarily ousted the new governor. In 1654 a Puritan assembly repudiated the proprietor, abrogated the Toleration Act and, after a pitched battle, outlawed Catholicism. Maryland remained a royal colony until 1715 when a descendent of the proprietor converted again to Anglicanism and the proprietorship was restored to the Calvert family. Though Anglicanism was now established and there were harsh laws against Catholics, Catholicism had a Maryland base in the colonies for the remainder of the colonial period.

The other major colony not yet discussed (besides Virginia) was New York, acquired by England when the Duke of York seized New Netherland from the Dutch in 1664. By the terms of surrender, the Dutch Reformed Church was guaranteed its liberties. Since half of the inhabitants of the entire colony were English Calvinists, the Duke granted toleration to each congregation having legally ordained clergy. The Dutch Church faced competition after the Glorious Revolution when the Anglican Church was granted public tax support in the four important lower counties, now the New York City area. This was the slender basis for the Anglican claim to "establishment" in New York. As the heterogeneous population of this busy seaport grew, many other religious groups competed with the two established churches during the 18th century.

Three phenomena affected all the colonies during the 18th century: the Great Awakening, beginning in New England, and stimulating evangelisation elsewhere; Anglican efforts to establish episcopacy in the colonies; and the Enlightenment.

One of the major contributors to the Great Awakening was the much-travelled George Whitefield, the English colleague of the Wesleys who first served as an Anglican chaplain in the new colony of Georgia. His successful activity in the South resulted in seven transatlantic preaching tours covering all the major colonies. He was invited to preach in New England by Jonathan Edwards, the learned Congregationalist already deviating from rigid Puritanism. Whitefield's powerful eloquence and his developing Calvinist inclinations appealed to many strict Congregationalists already unhappy with the lukewarm condition of established Congregationalism. Many set up separate congregations partly to restore religious discipline, and partly to take advantage of the toleration recently accorded Baptists, Anglicans and Quakers.

A major element of the Great Awakening and the evangelistic revivals in the South, abetted by Separate Baptist missionaries from New England, was an immense broadening of the field of preaching to attract common people, both the widely scattered settlers of the frontier and ordinary folk in the more settled areas. Though the religious message was fundamentalist, it not only awakened their receptivity to purely religious concerns but, as time passed, made common cause with those influenced by the Enlightenment on the political issues of church-state relations and toleration.

Presbyterians and Baptists as well as Congregationalists were split over revivalism. Baptists opposing it as unseemly—including the older groups—were dubbed Old Lights, whereas the proponents, who reaped the resulting harvest, were New Lights. Presbyterians underwent the same division, Old Side versus New Side.

Among the educated classes, the new look in religion was more intellectual, the result of rationalism imported from the English and European Enlightenment. Thomas Jefferson and his younger contemporary James Madison stand as examples of deism, though neither actually quit the Anglican Church. Even John Adams moved far from orthodox Calvinism, but not enough to wish to disturb the Congregational establishment's tax support. The impact of the Enlightenment has been described as "peaceful penetration" of the educated portion of the American religious spectrum.[29]

A religio-political issue which has been characterized as one of the two major causes of the American Revolution was the long struggle of the Anglican Church to establish episcopacy in the colonies.[30] As early as 1700, the Rev. Thomas Bray, who served briefly as Anglican Commissary in Maryland, saw the need for more and better Anglican clergy in the colonies and vigorously propagandized for this cause. The formation of the Society for the Propagation of the Gospel in Foreign Parts (SPG), chartered in 1702, was largely a result of Bray's efforts. The Anglican problem was not only to improve the number and caliber of clergy in the southern colonies where the church was established, but also to send aggressive missionaries to assist and carry forward the feeble Anglican foothold in the middle and New England colonies. The SPG's goals coincided with the late Stuarts' desire to bring the American colonies politically under more control by converting proprietorships to royal colonies. Bray's effort to create an American bishopric was on the verge of final authorization when Queen Anne died, but the advent under George I of the Whigs, who owed their power to dissenters, nullified the SPG's efforts for the while.

A more formidable effort began in mid century with the accession of the Rev. Thomas Sherlock as Bishop of London, in which capacity he not only had a seat on the Board of Trade and Plantations overseeing colonial affairs but was also president of the SPG, enjoying the patronage of the Archbishop of Canterbury. Appeals from SPG missionaries and a few of the laity in the middle colonies for a resident bishop were hampered not only by official caution in England but by the complete lack of any national or regional connection of the Anglicans in each colony with others, and the almost complete disinterest of Anglicans in the South.

The episcopacy issue was fueled by the measures undertaken by George III's ministers in the 1760's to impose the Stamp Act. The "plot" to install Anglican bishops in America was seen by colonists as part and parcel of the growing menace posed to their basic political liberties. Even the height of the outcry over the Stamp Act did not divert attention from the episcopal threat, including the possibility of taxation for support of bishops and creation of ecclesiastical courts. After the onset of the political agitation immediately preceding the Revolution, the episcopacy issue was for practical purposes irrelevant, though the Archbishop of Canterbury maintained pressure on its behalf until his death in 1781.

At the outbreak of the Revolution nine of the thirteen colonies contained established churches, whether through recognition of a state church, as in Virginia and Massachusetts, or through special advantages granted for one church. Dissenters had gained ground steadily since the Great Awakening in New England and the revivals elsewhere, and they gained a measure of tolerance in most states. In Massachusetts and Connecticut the Baptists, profiting from the Congregational Separatist movement, had gained considerable strength and, along with Episcopalians and Quakers, were now tolerated to the extent of being able to designate church taxes for their own clergy. Baptists had also made inroads in Virginia and further south, particularly since the former frontier, the Piedmont, was now considered part of the settled area as the frontier had moved west. In the Piedmont Baptist gains were strong and of increasing importance in applying pressure for toleration in Virginia.[31]

Virginia was an example of the trend toward toleration in a colony having an established church as well as the setting for the ideas of George Mason and others of the revolutionary generation in Virginia interested in church-state relations, especially Thomas Jefferson, James Madison and Patrick Henry. The Anglican establishment, which had endured more than a century and a half when the American Revolution erupted, remained relatively stable throughout that long period, but inevitably was affected by and interacted with developments in England and in the other colonies.

The first Virginia charter, granted to the Virginia Company of London in 1607, emphasized missions to the Indians in the form of "true Knowledge and Worship of God," with the

Church of England understood as the fount of true knowledge and worship.[32] The Second Charter issued three years later provided that all immigrants must take the Oath of Supremacy, thus screening out Catholic settlers. The Virginia Company assumed responsibility for sending and supporting Anglican clergy, and regular church attendance was to be required.[33]

In the troubled early years there were severe penalties for profanity, blasphemy and speaking against "the knowne articles of the Christian faith." The first representative assembly in the New World, the Virginia House of Burgesses established in 1619, mandated church services in Anglican form every Sunday, with fines for non-attendance. When the Company charter was revoked in 1624, the new royal governor was instructed to ensure observance of the Anglican service every Sunday and to assure adequate maintenance for the clergy.

The Virginia Church establishment which emerged during the 17th century was clearly modeled on Tudor and Stuart precedents. All inhabitants had to pay tithes and attend church, or pay a fine. Each clergyman was entitled to glebe land for his economic support, usually by growing and selling tobacco. Construction of churches was financed by local taxes. Church wardens and vestrymen were authorized, and the church structure, based on parishes, generally resembled that in England except for the absence of a bishop who could ordain and supervise all clergy and confirm communicants. The Bishop of London was represented administratively at Williamsburg by a Commissary, who held a seat on the Governor's Council.

Toleration of dissenters was another matter. Puritan clergymen who strayed into the colony were banished for failure to conform to Anglican rites, and all Quakers were fined, imprisoned and banished. No Catholic could hold public office, and any infiltrating priests were banished. As a further handicap for dissenters, all infants were to be christened in the Anglican Church.

As Puritans in England hardened their opposition to the established church under the persecution policy of Charles I and Archbishop Laud, they were persecuted as well in Virginia, and many fled to North Carolina. During the Cromwellian period a Puritan governor ruled Virginia and laws were passed increasing civil control of the church. One law turned over ecclesiastical affairs of the parishes to the vestries and people, as was being done in England. The Puritan rulers of Virginia were very harsh in their treatment of the Quakers; a law of 1659 ordered their imprisonment upon arrival, and fined all who gave them aid and comfort.

When the Restoration ended the Puritan rule of Virginia, active persecution of Quakers declined, though they were legally held responsible for paying tithes and penalized for refusing to take oaths or perform military service. New royal instructions to the restored Governor William Berkeley stated that Anglican services would again be required in the colony, but "because we are willing to give all possible encouragement to persons of different persuasions in matters of Religion to transport themselves thither . . . You are not to suffer any man to be molested or disquieted in the exercise of his Religion, so he be content with a quiet and peaceable enjoying it, and not therein giving offence or scandall to the Government."[34] Berkeley ignored these instructions and promoted even more stringent laws against nonconformists: no clergy except those ordained by an English bishop would be permitted in the colony and the right to perform valid marriage services was limited to Anglican clergy.

These laws accelerated the departure of many Puritan residents and worsened the already deplorable religious and moral climate of the colony, partly attributable to the widely scattered plantation settlements. In the late 17th century it was estimated that only a fifth of the parishes were supplied with clergy, and many of these were morally lax and ecclesiastically incompetent. Widespread contempt for the Anglican clergy by Anglican laymen as well as nonconformists was to prove a major factor in the later church-state separation issue.

Although Virginia officially ignored the Toleration Act of 1689 accompanying the Glorious Revolution in England, the legislature was finally compelled a decade later to license a Presbyterian clergyman to preach. Small groups of English Baptists had settled unmolested in the southeast and in the Blue Ridge in the early 18th century, and Lutheran and Reformed Germans from Pennsylvania now moved into the Valley, remote from Anglican control. Governor William Gooch, recognizing the need to develop and strengthen the frontier, readily acceded to a request in 1738 from the Philadelphia Synod, the major Presbyterian ecclesiastical authority in the colonies, to liberalize conditions for Presbyterians in Hanover County north of Richmond by acknowledging their rights under the Act of Toleration. The Hanover Presbytery became the ecclesiastical center for all the widely scattered Presbyterians throughout the province, including numerous Scotch-Irish streaming south in the 1730's from Pennsylvania into the Piedmont and the Valley. These were welcomed as a means of strengthening Virginia's frontier barrier against the Indians and against hostile French operating in the Ohio region.

George Mason's initial interest in toleration was stimulated by his desire to profit from the purchase and resale of the western lands in the Ohio River area, recognized by the original Virginia charter as part of the colony. The Ohio Company of Virginia was joined in 1749 by Mason, who became its treasurer for many years. He was allied with his uncle John Mercer in this venture. When a merchant travelling on behalf of the company to Europe to recruit settlers for the company's western holdings asked what inducements he might offer, the

Ohio Company Committee, which included Mason and Mercer, drafted a proposal in 1752 to settle foreign Protestants on their land with religious and economic advantages they might not find elsewhere. Concerning religion, the proposal stated: ". . . all foreign Protestants may depend on enjoying in this Government the Advantage of the Acts of Toleration in as full and ample measure as in any other of his Majesties plantations whatsoever, as great numbers of them have already experienced."[35]

Still, toleration was the exception, not the rule. Another wave of persecutions occurred in the late 1760's primarily in reaction to the violence of speech, and sometimes of action, by Separate Baptists recently settling in large numbers in the Piedmont. Many of their clergy were illiterate and unrestrained in their assaults on the establishment, partly because other sects such as Quakers, Moravians and Mennonites had now been exempt from licensing. Baptists in several regions were beaten, imprisoned and otherwise harassed for a decade largely because of a traditionalist, especially Anglican, fear of the social as well as religious consequences of the Great Awakening.[36]

When the Anglican Commissary asked the advice of Attorney General Peyton Randolph on dealing with the Baptist agitation in Spotsylvania County, the latter warned the royal attorney in Fredericksburg to this effect: ". . . the Act of Toleration (it being found by experience that persecuting dissenters increases their numbers) has given them a right to apply, in a proper manner, for licensed houses, for the worship of God according to their consciences; and I persuade myself, the gentlemen will quietly overlook their meetings, till the Court."[37]

In 1772 the House of Burgesses considered new legislation after Baptist petitions requested the same liberty as other Protestants. The legislative discussions included the difference between freedom as a natural right and toleration as a liberty granted by the state, an argument found among the Commonwealthmen in England. The bill finally proposed continued requirements for regulation, but no action was taken. In 1775 the General Assembly of Baptists petitioned the Burgesses for disestablishment, but the approach of revolution by this time had diverted legislative attention.[38]

Disillusionment with the Anglican clergy as a body came to a head in the "Parson's Cause" when the clergy protested the Two-Penny Act of 1758. Clergy salaries had been fixed a decade before at 16,000 pounds of tobacco annually, which could be sold at a good market rate and yield a comfortable income. A combination of crop failures and heavy taxes resulting from the French and Indian War of the mid-1750s led the assembly to enact that temporarily all debts payable in tobacco could be paid in cash at two pence per pound, a much lower rate; this would reduce current clergy income by two-thirds. The prime test came in Hanover County when a court declared the 1758 law invalid because it lacked royal approval and ordered a jury to determine damages against the plaintiff at the next court term. Counsel for the defense resigned, and in desperation the defendant turned to an unknown young lawyer of the area, Patrick Henry, whose eloquence made of the "Parson's Cause" a *cause célèbre.* Henry's argument diverted the point to a question of royal arrogance having overruled a just law designed to relieve distressed subjects. The jury brought in a verdict setting damages at only one penny. This case put the Anglican clergy in the worst possible light. It also propelled Patrick Henry into the limelight.[39]

The question of establishing an Anglican bishop in the colonies arose seriously in Virginia only in 1771, when an energetic Commissary, the Rev. James Horrocks, summoned a meeting of the provincial clergy at Williamsburg to consider the matter. Only a dozen were present, indicative of the general lack of enthusiasm among the Anglican clergy, in colonies where the church was established, for close-range episcopal supervision of their way of life. A motion to petition the king for a bishop was rejected, and the substitute idea of circulating a petition for signatures was carried only against vehement opposition. One argument of opponents was that an episcopate, seen as royal encroachment, would create a disturbance in all the colonies reminiscent of the recent Stamp Act commotion. It was particularly feared that such a move would stir up dissenter reaction in Virginia.[40]

Thus, on the eve of the Revolution George Mason, after years of service as a justice of the peace and a parish vestryman in Fairfax County, had seen ample evidence of the fruits of establishment and intolerance. Young James Madison as well, after his education at the College of New Jersey, contrasting the religious situation in Virginia with the freer atmosphere there, was intellectually prepared to put an end to the legal basis for intolerance.[41] The Virginia Declaration of Rights manifested their intentions.

Press and Speech in the Colonies

Suppression of free speech in the colonies antedated the establishment of the press and probably stemmed less from the courts than from communities and their elected representatives, especially the colonial assemblies. In 1660 the Virginia House of Burgesses committed a man for "scandalous, mutinous, and seditious" words criticizing the House on a tax matter. Normally seditious remarks were tried before local justices of the peace, and only serious cases affecting the state came to the Council's attention.[42]

In 1671, Governor Berkeley, replying to a query from the Lords Commissioners of Foreign Plantations concerning religion in Virginia, stated ". . . I thank God, there are no free schools nor *printing*, and I hope we shall not have these hundred years; for *learning* has brought disobedience, and heresy, and sects into the world, and *printing* has divulged them, and libels against the best government. . . ."[43]

William Penn presided over a Council meeting in 1683 ordering that the laws of Pennsylvania not be printed. Several cases in Pennsylvania involved William Bradford, who later played a role in the famous Zenger case in New York. Bradford's first publication, an almanac, was censored in manuscript and he was warned "not to print anything but what will have Lycence from ye Councill." In 1689 Bradford was in trouble for printing, at a councilor's request, a copy of the "Frame of Government" of 1682. His defense that he knew of no one appointed "Imprimator" or licenser was overruled by the Governor: "Sir, I am 'Imprimator' and that you shall know . . . I have particular order from Governor Penn for the suppressing of printing here, and narrowly to look after your press. . . ." This so dismayed Bradford that he returned briefly to England, but was soon back in Pennsylvania and in trouble. His press was seized and he was jailed on a charge of seditious libel. This has been described as "probably the first criminal trial in America involving freedom of the press."[44]

The development of the political force represented by the press and public opinion in the colonies was comparatively rapid, considering the cultural lag to be expected from a much smaller population settling the seaboard of a continental wilderness several months distant from the mother country. Of the various opinion-shaping media formats—the broadside, the pamphlet, and the newspaper—the last was most influential both because of its regularity and its mixture of opinion and reported events.

After 1690, date of the first newspaper in the largest colonial town, Boston, periodic journalism spread in the early 18th century at the rate of several newspapers per decade in the major seaports and such other provincial capitals as Annapolis and Williamsburg. The *Maryland Gazette* (founded 1727) and the first *Virginia Gazette* (founded 1736) were both of personal interest to George Mason. By mid-century, migrating printers, sometimes several members of the same family, created in effect a media network, each unit of which frequently reprinted articles of opinion as well as information found in other papers arriving in the embryonic postal system.[45]

Prior restraint of publication by the licensing requirement ended in the colonies in the early 1730's, though it had legally if not in practice ended in England when the Printing Act expired in the last century. King George I had instructed the Governor of Massachusetts in 1721 to enforce prior licensing of publications, but when the governor sought legislative endorsement, the Assembly refused, chiding him instead for permitting libels against itself. At stake was the Assembly's desire to wrest exclusive licensing control from the colony's executive, just as Parliament had done in England. The final attempt to enforce licensing in Massachusetts involved Benjamin Franklin's older brother, James, founder of the unlicensed *New England Courant* which was filled with political and religious satire. Publication of what the Council called "a high affront to this Government" resulted in censure and an order to print nothing without prior approval of the Secretary of the Province. James thereupon turned the *Courant* over to Benjamin to circumvent the order and thus made possible the latter's initial success as a printer.[46]

The most sensational attack on the court procedures in seditious libel cases in the colonies, and one which also attracted attention in England, was the case of John Peter Zenger in New York.[47] As a result of his difficulties in Pennsylvania, William Bradford had migrated to New York and established the *New-York Gazette* as the licensed organ of the colony's administration. Becoming wealthy and conservative in old age, he criticized Zenger in 1733 for publishing "pieces tending to set the province in a flame, and to raise seditions and tumults."

The New York Weekly Journal was established in 1733 as an alternative to Bradford's *New-York Gazette*, the mouthpiece for the new and already unpopular royal governor William Cosby, and thereby was "the first politically independent newspaper in America." In 1738 Cosby and his Council requested Assembly concurrence in ordering four issues of the *Journal* publicly burnt, offering a reward for the apprehension of the unknown authors of articles tending to raise "Seditions and Tumults among the People," and prosecuting the offending printer, Zenger. The Assembly tabled the proposal but the Council put the measures into effect anyway. Zenger was arrested, jailed for seditious libel and held incommunicado. His attorneys obtained a writ of habeas corpus but bail was set so high that Zenger languished in jail while his wife carried on the *Journal*. Of Zenger's two attorneys, one, James Alexander, was editor of the *Journal* and rich in legal and political experience. They argued that two of the three Supreme Court justices sitting as a court of first instance were improperly appointed by the governor without advice and consent of the Council. The Chief Justice promptly disbarred both attorneys and assigned a pro-administration lawyer as defense counsel.

Zenger's erstwhile attorneys sought other counsel for Zenger outside of New York and not subject to peremptory disbarment. They finally persuaded the respected Andrew Hamilton of Philadelphia, former attorney general of Pennsylvania and speaker of the Pennsylvania Assembly, to assume the role. There had been an incident concerning the press in Pennsylvania a few years earlier when Hamilton was a member of the provincial Council.[35] The Council had summoned Andrew Bradford (son of William Bradford and founder of

Pennsylvania's first newspaper in 1720) for printing criticisms of the province's declining credit. The Governor and Court ordered that there be no more publication concerning the affairs of Pennsylvania or any other colonial government without official permission. Apparently Hamilton's outlook had changed by the time he was asked to defend Zenger.[48]

Hamilton had both an English case and a 17th century Pennsylvania trial to cite as defense precedents; ironically the latter was one of the Pennsylvania cases against William Bradford! When initial argument for truth as sufficient defense was rejected by the court, Hamilton admitted the fact of publication and argued that the jury should decide on law as well as facts. The jury returned a verdict of "not guilty."

Hamilton, a supreme tactician, became famous in the colonies and in England partly because of Alexander's published account of the trial, termed by one authority as with the possible exception of *Cato's Letter*, "the most widely known source of libertarian thought in England and America during the eighteenth century." Alexander's hitherto obscure role has been recently enhanced by appreciation for his essay on freedom of speech replying to attacks upon the Zenger defense. He enunciated as a first principle: "Freedom of speech is a *principal Pillar* in a free Government; when this Support is taken away, the Constitution is dissolved, and Tyranny is erected on its ruins . . . abuses of Freedom of Speech are the excrescences of Liberty. They ought to be suppressed; but to whom dare we commit the care of doing it?" Though he rather lamely concluded that the means of protecting freedom of speech was truth as defense, he has been hailed as the first colonial figure to develop a philosophy of freedom of speech-and-press.[49] This coincides with the view of Franklin and other leaders that writer and printer remained liable for the truth of what was printed.

In the southern states, the governor's councils and lower

Houses were as zealous as the governors to suppress criticism of any sort. In George Mason's Virginia, the Burgesses prosecuted a William and Mary professor, an Anglican clergyman, for saying privately in 1758 that during the "Parson's Cause" case he would refuse to administer the sacrament to any "Scoundrels" in the legislature who voted to settle salaries of the clergy in cash instead of tobacco. Arrested, he was forced to beg pardon for questioning the honor of the Burgesses. On the other hand, the founder of the first *Virginia Gazette*, William Parks, was acquitted of a charge of seditious libel of a Burgess after proving in court that the Burgess had in fact once been convicted of sheep-stealing as alleged.

The colonial press came into its own as a major political force early in the reign of George III when the London government sought to reorganize and tighten its control over the American colonies.[50] Resentment of previous stamp taxes affecting the press in New England during the Seven Years War had not faded completely early in 1765, when passage of the Stamp Act raised a storm of protest throughout the colonies. The new act bore hard on the press, since all aspects of the printing trade were taxed: raw materials, apprentice labor, sale of the final product, and the other principal revenue source, advertising. To make ends meet publishers were forced to raise subscription rates—always difficult to collect—and lost many subscribers in the process. Many papers defied the act and continued publishing without stamped paper.

But not all printers suffered heavily, and several new papers were established during the Stamp Act crisis. Public interest in news about developments in the colonists' relationship with Britain whetted the appetite for newspapers, and their number almost doubled, from 49 in 1763 to 82 in 1775.[51]

The multiplication of papers is abundantly illustrated in Virginia. The original *Virginia Gazette*, taken over in 1765 by Alexander Purdie, was briefly suspended during the crisis but revived under the joint management of Purdie and John Dixon. Purdie left the partnership in 1775 to establish his own *Virginia Gazette.* Meanwhile, in 1766, as a result of the Stamp Act crisis, prominent Virginia Whigs, dissatisfied with the impartiality exhibited by the original *Gazette* under Purdie, had invited William Rind from Annapolis to establish a *Gazette* reflecting Whig views. Still another paper, the *Virginia Gazette and Norfolk Intelligencer,* enjoyed a brief existence in 1774–1775 until its press was seized by Lord Dunmore when the Revolution erupted in Virginia.[52]

In Virginia, George Mason had been personally embarrassed by the appointment of a relative as stamp agent, and others had been devising means of resisting the Stamp Act even before it came into effect. Mason's use of the press as a political forum began in 1766 with his irritation with the tone of a letter from British merchants to merchants in New York urging moderation in their reaction to the stamp tax and printed in Purdie's *Virginia Gazette* in May. He wrote an angry letter to a London paper castigating the British attitude toward the colonists and stressing the absurdity of trying to enforce the Stamp Act by military power. By mid-May a nonimportation agreement was organized for Virginia at Williamsburg.[53]

The colonial press was congratulated and congratulated itself upon its significant role in such crises. Aside from some journals having firm ties to colonial administrators and a few others with unsympathetic editors or publishers, most of the press moved immediately into the role of defenders of American liberties. The papers in the New England and Middle colonies were the most vociferous in opposition, but major journals in the South also joined in. Editors and printers felt much less inhibited than before by the legal penalties, which now seemed less likely to be invoked. The avowedly partisan press had begun to replace the earlier stance of impartiality, and on the eve of the Revolution "liberty of the press" was being defined as liberty only to support the patriot cause.[54]

This situation continued during the Revolution and in its patriotic afterglow, so that further discussion of press and speech prior to the Bill of Rights is not warranted here.

After 1776: Separation of Church and State in Virginia

The newly independent state's leaders, except for a few serving with the army in the North, were too busy organizing the new state government and taking military and economic steps for waging war to bother with implementing the "free exercise of religion" as provided in the Declaration of Rights.[55]

In the first session of the legislature in 1776 after independence was declared, petitions arrived from Presbyterian and Baptist dissenters in several quarters of the state asking relief from religious taxation, and condemning the continuation of the established church. Most hailed Article 16 of the Declaration of Rights as the basis for their renewed pleas. The House of Delegates, as the lower house was now titled, had established a committee on religion to which the petitions were referred. Fresh from his leading role in declaring independence at Philadelphia, Thomas Jefferson was a member, but Mason had not yet arrived and was not included.

In the committee Jefferson presented a resolution calling for repeal of all laws passed in Britain or Virginia which in any way restricted freedom of belief or worship and for the repeal of all laws establishing the Anglican Church in Virginia. He argued that state intrusion into religion was a violation of natural rights, since men entering the social compact had surrendered only their rights necessary for civil government. Conservative maneuvers to scuttle Jefferson's proposals resulted in a compromise leaving the established Church in place but repealing all laws requiring church attendence and direct taxation of dissenters for support. Mason persuaded the House to agree to repeal any British act "which renders criminal the maintaining of any Opinions in matters of Religion, forbearing to repair to Church, or the exercising any mode of worship whatever. . . ." British but not Virginia laws were affected.[56]

Although this initial effort to separate church and state relieved dissenters to some extent, it contained a clause leaving open the question of a general assessment or voluntary contribution for the public support of religion. This was to occasion much difficulty before the final statute for religious liberty was accepted in 1785.

The war again preempted the Delegates' attention until 1779, when Jefferson reintroduced a version of his bill for religious liberty as a part of the general revision of the Virginia laws ordered in 1776. The bill was quietly shelved by the House. Agitation for and against it between sessions continued, and when the fall session began, Mason was a member of the committee which drafted a bill "concerning religion," though it is unlikely he would have agreed with its final proposals. Modelled on the religious section of the South Carolina Constitution of 1778, it would have restricted toleration to individuals and groups subscribing to the Protestant Christian religion and acknowledging the necessity for public worship. Religious groups would be supported by an enforced general assessment.

The South Carolina experiment, however, was already known to be in difficulty, and the Delegates finally awoke to the fact that the bill they were on the verge of passing would nullify the important religious article of the Declaration of Rights. It was effectively buried by postponement to the next session. Mason and two other delegates were then ordered to submit a bill repealing a Virginia statute providing salaries for the Anglican clergy. They presented it with a preamble stating that "the people would never again be compelled to contribute to the Support or Maintenance of the former established Church." The bill was passed but without the preamble, a harbinger of difficult battles ahead over a general assessment. Minor concessions to dissenters included liberalizing the marriage laws.

Cornwallis' invasion of Virginia in 1780, during which Jefferson's term as governor expired ingloriously as the government fled the capital, again diverted public and official attention from the religious question until 1783. Mason retired from the legislature at the end of the 1780 term. Patrick Henry, whose oratorical skill had propelled him to a powerful position in the House, was disturbed by the general decline in morality and he was now receptive to the new wave of postwar petitions for a general assessment to support religion. As petitions favoring assessment continued to flow in, Madison's lucid arguments against the measure were futile in the face of Henry's fervent support, and only Henry's election to the governorship averted almost certain passage. Arguments continued for weeks without result until the assessment bill was finally postponed until the next session to allow public review of the matter.

In the meantime opponents could marshal their resources. Several pro-assessment legislators were ousted in the spring elections. Presbyterian as well as Baptist opposition was increasingly apparent, since the former were hearing from their numerous anti-assessment brethren in the Valley. The Episcopal Church, incorporated as successor to the established church under this name, was preoccupied with proposed changes in doctrine and liturgy, a proposal for national organization of their Church and effects of the formal separation from them in 1784 of the Methodists, who had hitherto supported the church's position.

In the summer of 1785, urged on by George Mason and others, Madison composed his famed *Memorial and Remonstrance*, basing freedom of conscience on natural right. Mason took a leading role in supporting the Remonstrance at the grassroots level by having quantities printed as a petition for circulation in Northern Virginia.[57] By the time the legislature convened in October only 10 percent of the more than 100 petitions on the matter favored assessment. In addition, a sharp decline in the post-war economic boom made it clear that any new tax, including an assssment for religion, would now be politically infeasible.

The legislature was ready to take up again the general post-independence revision of the laws, and Jefferson's bill on religion was among those to be considered. After speedy passage of many of the revisionary bills, opposition arose to further consideration and particularly to the bill for religious liberty. Moves to narrow or eliminate Jefferson's eloquent preamble and to postpone the bill until the next session were defeated and it passed December 17 by a wide margin. The more conservative Senate passed the bill with amendments to the preamble but left intact the final clause of the bill declaring that the rights guaranteed by the bill belonged to the "natural rights of mankind" and that any future attempt to repeal or limit the provisions of the bill would violate those rights. In a joint conference, both houses agreed on further amendments, the major one of which struck from the preamble the statement that "the religious opinions of men are not the object of civil government, nor under its jurisdiction." Even Madison felt compelled to support this change lest the bill be further delayed or even postponed. The House speaker signed it on January 19, 1785. Madison reaped political credit at home and Jefferson was congratulated by his European friends on this triumph of reason. That its basis lay in Mason's Virginia Declaration of Rights was not made explicit but was nevertheless true. Throughout the struggle for passage Mason had proved his adherence to the principle of religious liberty as defined in the Declaration of Rights.

The Episcopal Church was not yet severed completely from the state, even though the same session of the Delegates had passed a bill shifting responsibility for parish poor from vestries to civil officials. Other struggles remained, since dissenters generally resented the recent incorporation of the Episcopal Church, particularly the transfer to it of all churches and land formerly held by the established church. They reasoned that since public funds had paid for these properties, they should revert to the public. Much further wrangling ensued and this issue was not fully resolved until 1802. By then the pro-separation Baptists and Methodists had become a majority, and the actual as well as legal separation of church and state in Virginia as well as at the national level was guaranteed.

Mason, the Constitution, and the Bill of Rights

The articles of Confederation by definition could have no impact on individual rights in the 13 states comprising the confederation. The Congress operating under the Articles, however, recognized the need to guarantee individual rights in the large northwestern territories ceded to the central government by the seaboard states claiming the northwest lands by charter, particularly Virginia.

In its resolution of 1780 designed to encourage the states' cession of western lands to the United States, Congress had promised that all ceded lands would, when settled, be formed into separate states with a republican form of government which would enter the union with the same rights of sovereignty, freedom and independence as the original states. In

1787, Congress made good on its promises with respect to future states and buttressed these with a list of individual rights for the inhabitants which has been characterized as the "first bill of rights enacted by the federal government of the United States." Following the lengthy sections devoted to the form and powers of the territorial government pending the organization of separate states, the first of six articles concerning rights was a succinct statement concerning religion: "No person, demeaning himself in a peaceable and orderly manner, shall ever be molested on account of his mode of worship, or religious sentiments, in the said territory." The Northwest Ordinance was passed by the Confederation Congress in July, 1787, just a few weeks after the Philadelphia Convention had assembled.[58]

During the early period of operation of the Articles of Confederation Mason seemed satisfied with them as a sufficiently close national bond, and saw no reason to extend their scope in the manner advocated by his neighbor, Washington. Mason's views were forcefully set forth in Fairfax County's instructions to its Assembly delegates: "We desire and instruct you strenuously to oppose all encroachments of the American Congress upon the sovereignty and jurisdiction of the separate States; and every assumption of power, not expressly vested in them, by the Articles of Confederation. . . ."[59]

Characteristically, Mason's slowly developing interest in strengthening the central government had a local and personal basis: the long dispute over the boundary and fishing and navigation rights on the Potomac between Virginia and Maryland, simmering since Maryland was carved early in the 17th century out of what Virginia regarded as its rightful territory. There had been continual friction during the Revolution concerning defense of this vital waterway, and the revival of trade after hostilities had ended increased the mutual desire for settlement. Mason was one of the five Virginians appointed to negotiate with Maryland representatives. In late March 1785 he and another Virginia commissioner met the Marylanders and were invited by Washington to meet at Mount Vernon. Terms of a bi-state agreement were worked out and transmitted by Mason and his Virginia colleague to the Assembly, together with an appeal to the president of the Pennsylvania Council describing plans for an extension of the negotiations to cover proposed water and road routes westward from the Potomac to the Ohio.[60] Similar action was under way in Maryland.

Out of this affair grew the idea for a still broader conference at Annapolis in 1786 to consider and recommend measures to improve trade of the United States as a whole. The better-known Annapolis Convention attracted representatives from only five states; rather than consider probably futile measures, the assembled delegates voiced their unanimous wish for a speedy general meeting of all the States with a view to "extending the powers of their Deputies, to other objects than those of Commerce. . . ." Thus, as is well remembered, was born the Philadelphia Convention of 1787.

Mason and Madison were the only two Virginians appointed to all three of the successive meetings culminating in the federal constitution. Mason had been unable to attend the Annapolis Convention because of illness and accepted appointment to the Philadelphia Convention with great reluctance. His age, health and dislike of travel were overcome only by the sense of duty which had previously brought him to the Virginia Assembly at critical times. Of the original Virginia appointees, Patrick Henry, "smelling a rat," declined, and another previous rights ally, Richard Henry Lee, refused an invitation to replace Henry on the grounds that a member of the Confederation Congress should not also sit in the Convention. Governor Edmund Randolph, who proved to be a staunch Mason ally during the Convention, was appointed, along with the venerable George Wythe, Washington and Madison, known advocates of a stronger central government. They were joined by two others, John Blair and Dr. James McClurg.[61]

Both of the plans for union presented at Philadelphia—those submitted by Virginia and New Jersey—were concerned with the balance of power between large and small states; neither mentioned individual rights. Nevertheless at an early point Mason, fearful of a dangerously strong role for a national government, urged the Convention to consider the rights of citizens. Admitting that "we had been too democratic," he was equally fearful of a reaction to the opposite extreme, and he urged the Convention to "attend to the rights of every class of the people." He hoped they would "provide no less carefully for the rights—and happiness of the lower than the highest orders of citizens." On this point Madison and the Pennsylvanian James Wilson, who later opposed a bill of rights as unnecessary, agreed with Mason, but Elbridge Gerry of Massachusetts, later Mason's strongest convention ally, objected that the people were "dupes of pretended patriots" and required checks on their freedom.

Obviously, roles in the Convention had not hardened, nor could they at this stage. On June 20 when Mason averred he would never agree to abolish state governments or "render them insignificant," as Alexander Hamilton favored, Charles Pinckney of South Carolina at this point professed no reason for alarm. He expected state governments to preserve his rights. Weeks later in July when the problem of defining and electing a chief executive came up, Mason reiterated his creed: "The pole star of his political conduct" was "the preservation of the rights of the people." Without comment the Convention adjourned to leave preparation of a draft constitution to a Committee of Detail.

In the Committee's report, which kept the delegates busy

into September, the powers accorded the central government aroused apprehensions in some minds concerning personal liberties. On August 20 Pinckney submitted propositions to meet such needs, including a significant one for banning religious tests for any federal office holder. Finding his list not acceptable as a whole to the Convention, he, Mason, and Gerry took the lead in trying to insert piecemeal its provisions and others which they favored. The proposal for the ban on religious tests for office, accepted over the objections of Roger Sherman of Connecticut that it was "unnecessary," survived as the sole reference to religion in the final Constitution text. Pinckney and Gerry joined in demanding a statement "that the liberty of the Press shall be inviolably preserved," but Sherman's rejoinder that the "power of Congress does not extend to the press" reflected the majority view.

As part of their strategy Mason and Gerry also sought to postpone adoption of the article providing ratification of the constitution by state conventions specially elected for the purpose. Mason even suggested that, unless certain points in the draft concerning the federal government were settled in a manner satisfactory to those fearful for state sovereignty, he would wish the whole subject brought before another Convention to consider amendments proposed by the states.

At this point he began exchanging views in private meetings with Gerry, Luther Martin of Maryland, and others. On September 12 what he regarded as a final rebuff occurred after he emphatically expressed his desire that the constitution be "prefaced with a Bill of Rights . . . It would give great quiet to the people; and with the aid of the State Declarations of Rights a bill might be prepared in a few hours." Gerry moved and Mason seconded a motion for a committee to prepare a bill of rights. Once again Sherman attacked the idea of specifying rights by stating that "The State Declarations of Rights are not repealed by this Constitution; and being in force are sufficient," to which Mason rejoined, "The Laws of the United States are to be paramount to State Bills of Rights." In the vote on Gerry's motion, the Massachusetts delegation, though disagreeing with him, politely abstained but the rest of Virginia's delegation voted solidly against. All of the 10 voting states repudiated the idea.

On the day of Mason's rebuff, when the Committee of Style submitted its proposed final draft of the Constitution, he penned nine major objections to the proposed final draft of the Constitution, on his own copy.[62] The first concerned individual rights, noting the lack of a declaration of rights and suggesting that since the laws of the general government would be paramount, the declarations of rights of the separate states were no security. The last item in his listing of individual rights observed that there was no section preserving liberty of the press. There was no specific mention of freedom of religion, presumably considered covered by the general reference to a "bill of rights." Other important objections concerned the structure and scope of the proposed government. This list was the basis of George Mason's antiratification campaign.

In the final voting by clauses on the Committee of Style report, Mason participated actively, sometimes joined only by Randolph in disagreement. Historians have observed that Mason lost his convention image as a defender of individual rights at the very end when he tried to have another portion, already subject of a major compromise between northern and most southern states, changed by a motion to postpone any navigation acts before 1808 without a two-thirds majority. This was defeated but lingered in many delegates' minds later.

Refusing to sign the Constitution, along with Gerry and Edmund Randolph, Mason left Philadelphia. Luther Martin of Maryland, who later claimed he had for a time considered proposing a bill of rights, and two New Yorkers, John King and Robert Yates, had already left without signing. Mason's objections had failed at Philadelphia but were prophetic of the future when a Bill of Rights was finally submitted to the states by Congress and ratified by most, including Virginia.

A final effort to influence the Constitution before it was submitted to the states by Congress in New York was made by Virginia's representatives Richard Henry Lee and William Grayson.[63] Lee had visited Philadelphia during the Convention and learned of Mason's and other opponents' sentiments. When the Constitution reached New York, Lee tried to have the Congress reject it on the grounds that the Convention had exceeded its authority. When this failed, he argued in vain that Congress itself should make needed amendments. Finally, he suggested proposals to be added to the document when transmitted to state conventions. His list opened with the assertion that declarations of rights adopted by most states were evidence of the people's will concerning a bill of rights, and therefore there must be a federal bill to guarantee freedom of religion and freedom of the press along with other rights, including rights to assembly and petition not included in the Constitution text. This too was rejected, and the Constitution text went out to the states.

Mason, after a wearying trip home during which he was injured when his coach overturned, had his list of objections speedily printed as a pamphlet, in time to encourage opponents of ratification in the Pennsylvania legislature at the end of September when they "seceded" from the legislature because their criticisms were being overwhelmed. Lee's list of similar objections also circulated in Pennsylvania, and both lists undoubtedly were responsible for the issue of a minority report, following the ratification convention, which listed freedom of religion and freedom of speech and press.

As state ratifications proceeded, and the strength of the

antis in some conventions became evident, the need for compromise by federalists to pacify enough of the opposition to permit ratification became apparent.[64] Massachusetts led the way when, with Gerry present as an invited expert on the new constitution, chairman Samuel Adams unexpectedly indicated that he could support ratification provided a list of proposed amendments was forwarded with the ratification text. This pattern was followed by seven more of the twelve ratifying states. Six of their lists listed freedom of religion and five freedom of the press, with three of the latter adding freedom of speech.[65]

Eight state ratifications of the nine required for adoption had been completed by the spring of 1788. Of the remaining four states, the principal were Virginia and New York, both strategically important and, in the case of Virginia, still very wealthy and the most populous of the states.

As the Virginia convention opened on June 3, sentiment seemed too evenly divided to predict the outcome, and friends of the Constitution like Madison worried lest the antis might be the stronger. The power of anti leadership was not disputed; Patrick Henry's oratory was regarded as the most powerful in the state, and George Mason's stature as an elder statesman was formidable. However, Richard Henry Lee had declined election to the Convention, and Governor Edmund Randolph was known to be veering to the federalist position. Jefferson was at his post in France. The major gap in the federalist ranks was George Washington, deliberately aloof at Mount Vernon though his sentiments were evident and his influence an almost tangible presence. Young Madison's abilities for persuasive logical presentation were recognized. Not yet really convinced of the desirability of a bill of rights, he had recently been warned that Virginia Baptists were generally anti. Elder John Leland, a Baptist leader in Madison's Orange County home area, had prepared a written list of objections, especially concerning lack of a bill of rights guaranteeing freedom of religion and the press, which had been forwarded to Madison.

Once the Convention got underway Henry and Mason launched their offensive. Mason's advocacy of a bill of rights was known to all, and he spent most of his arguments on the other flaws he perceived in the text of the Constitution. Henry, who had never approved the idea of a national constitution, hammered continuously on the theme of the danger to civil liberties, especially freedom of conscience, freedom of the press and trial by jury in criminal as well as civil cases.

Virginia federalists finally realized, as others elsewhere had earlier, that the lack of a bill of rights seriously jeopardized prospects for ratification. George Wythe gave the cue for compromise when, as Convention time was running short, he submitted motions calling for ratification and for recommending amendments to be made following ratification. Specifically, Wythe listed freedom of the press and religion and guarantee of trial by jury. Henry immediately submitted 15 amendments, based on the views of the anti group. The final day of arguments turned on the question of whether amendments should be required before or after ratification. The original motion to ratify without amendments was passed 89–79.

To assuage the numerous antis, a committee to prepare proposed amendments was appointed, including Mason and Henry, and promptly reported a 20-article bill of rights plus 20 other articles listing perceived defects in the Constitution. The bill of rights was essentially Mason's Virginia Declaration of Rights, one major modification being the addition of the provision for freedom of speech in addition to that on freedom of the press, and, of course, freedom of religion.[66]

Madison's conversion to full support of a bill of rights was influenced by a lengthy and now famous correspondence with

Jefferson, still in France, and by his own problems in gaining election to the first Congress as a Virginia representative. He had particularly to reassure Baptist voters in his district. Keeping his word to the Virginia Convention antis, and despite the commotion attending organization of the new government, Madison announced on May 4, 1789, that he would soon bring up the subject of amendments to the Constitution.[67] On June 8 he presented a list of items distilled from the common elements of the proposals submitted by the individual states. In July the House decided to refer the matter to a select committee composed of one representative from each of the 11 states then represented and empowered to consider all the lists.[68]

The committee reported and Representative Richard Bland Lee of Virginia moved a committee of the whole to consider. The perennial opponent of a bill of rights, Sherman of Massachusetts, opposed, but Madison's anxiety was sufficient apparently to carry the motion.

His consolidated list drew heavily on the proposed Virginia amendments, based on the Declaration of Rights (which, after all, he had had a personal role in framing) augmented by ideas drawn from proposed amendments by all the states including others proposed by Virginia. His list was intended to be inserted into the text of the Constitution at appropriate points, with the items comprising individual rights to be placed in Article 1, Section 9, between clauses 3 and 4.

There were nine items in the "bill of rights" and freedom of religion headed them: "The civil rights of none shall be abridged on account of religious belief or worship, nor shall any national religion be established, nor shall the full and equal rights of conscience be in any manner, or on any pretext, infringed." The second item focused on freedom of speech as well as press: "The people shall not be deprived or abridged of their right to speak, or to write, or to publish their sentiments; and the freedom of the press, as one of the great bulwarks of liberty, shall be inviolable." Thus freedom of religion and of expression received even more emphasis than in the Virginia Declaration of Rights and in the comparable list of Virginia's proposed amendments. This reflects the consensus of most of the states which had either embodied them in their constitutions or discovered their importance in the ratification debates. Madison's full commitment to individual rights is evident in his effort to have Congress adopt an amendment making the Bill of Rights binding within each state, but this was roundly rejected.

The version which emerged from the select committee on July 28 retained the top rankings for religion, press and speech. The first item now read: "No religion shall be established by law, nor shall the equal rights of conscience be infringed." In the course of committee debate the qualifier "national" before religion had been deleted lest it connote too powerful a central government, and Madison had to calm New England fears that Congress could interfere with the Congregational state church. The second item on speech and press had been sharpened and augmented by references to assembly and petition: "The freedom of speech, and of the press, and the right of the people to assemble and consult for their common good, and to apply to the government for redress of grievances, shall not be infringed."

The House made a major change when it determined to have the proposed amendments remain a list of amendments rather than incorporate them into the text, apparently following the reasoning that a stable constitutional text with appended amendments was more seemly than a continually changing text. The completed House version included a total of 17 proposed amendments. Again, some variants of phrasing:

> Article the Third: Congress shall make no law establishing religion or prohibiting the free exercise thereof, nor shall the rights of Conscience be infringed.
> Article the Fourth: The Freedom of Speech, and of the Press, and the right of the people peaceably to assemble, and consult for their common good, and to apply to the Government for a redress of grievances, shall not be infringed.

It was the Senate which insisted on merging these vital elements:

> Congress shall make no law establishing articles of faith, or a mode of worship, or prohibiting the free exercise of religion, or abridging the freedom of speech, or of the press, or the right of the people peaceably to assemble, and to petition to the government for a redress of grievances.

After joint conference to resolve the differences between House and Senate treatment of the amendments, the First Amendment took its present form with modification of the religion part:

> Congress shall make no law respecting an establishment of religion, or prohibiting the free exercise thereof; or abridging the freedom of speech, or of the press; or the right of the people peaceably to assemble, and to petition the Government for a redress of grievances.

Prior to the Senate consideration Madison had received encouraging news of George Mason's personal reaction to the proposed amendments: "With two or three further Amendments . . . I could cheerfully put my Hand and Heart to the New Government."[69] The "further amendments" Mason wished did not pertain to civil liberties.

Twelve amendments were finally submitted by Congress to the states. The first two, concerning apportionment of seats in the House and the procedure for raising congressional salaries, were defeated everywhere. The remaining ten amendments concerning rights survived to become the national Bill of Rights.

With Vermont newly admitted to the union, ratification of the amendments by 11 of the 14 states was required to bring them into effect. Connecticut and Georgia, pronouncing the amendments unnecessary, did not ratify them and the Massachusetts legislature was long deadlocked in debate over the federal tax power. Therefore, Virginia's vote was crucial. The House of Delegates had approved the amendments in short order, but the conservative majority in the Senate stalled until spring elections in 1791 demonstrated public support of the amendments. Thus belatedly, on December 15, 1791, two months after George Mason had died quietly at Gunston Hall, Virginia ratification was completed and the Bill of Rights became part of the fundamental law of the land.[70]

Even before Mason's death his ideas were spreading abroad. In revolutionary France they influenced the Declaration of the Rights of Man and of the Citizen. Together, his Virginia Declaration of Rights and its two offspring, the American Bill of Rights and the French Declaration, have influenced constitutions all over the world.

The bicentennials of the ratification of the United States Constitution (1987) and Bill of Rights (1991) are fast approaching. To commemorate the role of George Mason in these events, a projected series of ten volumes, of which this is the second, is being published annually as "The George Mason Lectures." These are designed to examine the contributions of the man whose name George Mason University bears.

Prof. Robert Rutland, in the first 1983 lecture on "George

Mason and the Origins of the First Amendment," compared Mason's contemporary situation and American history up to the Civil War with today's plethora of civil rights legislation and litigation, and concludes that Mason and the Founding Fathers "thought the real purpose of the first amendment was to preserve our political—not our personal—freedom. . . . Mason was an agent for change. But that agency was on behalf of a general principle—not for the sake of a religious zealot's right to sell flowers in an airport or for an editor to have the right to defame a politician with impunity." He notes the impact of the humanistic Enlightenment which flourished among Virginia planters so that "Mason, Madison, Jefferson and Washington were the products of a system that exalted human reason, virtue and justice." To the contemporaries of Mason and Madison, the amendment seemed a way to preserve republican institutions by preventing governmental interference in the specified areas of religion, press, assembly, and petition. When Mason expressed satisfaction with the suggested amendments Madison had submitted to Congress, his recommendations for further amendments concerned the judiciary and commercial laws, not personal liberties.

The second lecture by Prof. Rosemary S. Keller, discussed the role of women in religion in the United States; she is collaborating on a multivolume series on this topic which is currently appearing. In her lecture on "The First Amendment: As Amended by the Founding Mothers" she traced the colonial background and precedents for the creation of a new kind of space or dimension in women's lives as strong-minded women, many more than we are accustomed to think, took significant steps to broaden religious concepts and practice from their women's viewpoint, despite the male view of women's proper place as subordinate to men.

After sketching the slender possibilities for such activity in the Spanish and French colonial Catholic churches in North

America and the efforts of all the major groups of settlers among the American Indians, she discussed the varying patterns and rates of development on women's activities in the diverse religious spectrum of the English colonies. The pattern and rate differed according to whether the dominant ethos was Puritan, Anglican, Baptist, Quaker or other, and was compounded throughout the South by the presence of many black slaves. There the evangelical impulse to bring all to salvation conflicted with the developing rigidity of Southern political and social attitudes and practices toward blacks. Because of Southern political and social attitudes and practices, Southern women found themselves at once elevated as the source of moral and religious influence but expected to confine themselves within home and family.

The same forces which produced the ferment leading to the American Revolution and to the enumeration of basic rights, especially the separation of church and state in constitutions during the revolutionary period, enabled American women in the nineteenth and twentieth centuries to take increasingly active and public roles in American religious life, even though excluded from the clergy until recent times.

Prof. Frederick Schauer, in "Free Speech and its Philosophical Roots," discussed freedom of the press as well as speech, noting that "George Mason, by being the principal author of the Virginia Declaration of Rights of 1776, was therefore the source of the world's first explicit legal protection of freedom of the press." He described the language of the First Amendment to the Constitution as "simple and bold" but "neither clear nor self-defining." He therefore sought guidance in the historical and philosophical approaches to throw light on its meaning today.

Historically, Mason's familiarity with the writings of "Cato", John Wilkes and Junius provides one clue: that fallible government requires checks. The value of a philosophical inquiry lies in the fact that "abstract language enables the Constitution to stand the test of time" but this is small comfort to the legislator or judge facing concrete situations. He or she finds little value in the search for the intent of the framers. While applicable to simple provisions, it is extremely difficult when dealing with such great abstractions as freedom of speech, press and religion. The fact that the words of the framers were ratified as a legal text, makes them authoritative in and of themselves. Thus it is reasonable for courts to interpret these generalities by working out theories of what the words can mean now.

Some of the prevalent theories do not hold up under scrutiny. The "search for truth" argument breaks down at the point where government has any role in deciding what may be true. The argument that individual freedom is promoted opens the door to an unlimited range of action and collapses into a general argument for personal liberty rather than for freedom of speech and press:

> The argument that grounds freedom of speech and freedom of the press in a particular distrust of governmental officials to deal with a certain kind of communication may not be the only argument for freedom of speech and press. . . There is no reason to suppose that freedom of speech and press must necessarily be one and only one principle, and it is quite likely that we are dealing with a collection of different principles that happen to be joined under the particular simplifying rubric that happens to be made for freedom of speech and press, and it is also the argument that is most able to explain the special position we grant to freedom of speech and press in our system of government and constitutional protection.

In order to decide some of the wide-ranging cases currently involving the courts under the rubric of free speech, we have to search for the foundations of the First Amendment, and then determine if the novel case at hand has anything to do with the reasons for having the First Amendment at all.

Charles William Maynes drew on his State Department experience and the insights gathered in editing the influential *Foreign Policy* magazine in discussing "American Foreign Policy and Human Rights: The New Realism." As a starting point he cited the classic statement by Sir Isaiah Berlin distinguishing "negative" from "positive" rights. American tradition favors the former, both domestically and abroad, but Maynes noted that both types can cover abuses, e.g., the long neglect of full civil rights for blacks in the United States. Though Americans tend to favor equality of opportunity rather than results, he suggested that "first amendment rights to a free press may not be terribly useful to a man who cannot read," and asked if this implies that the state therefore has a positive obligation to educate its citizens so they can exercise a "negative" right. He observed that although the Carter administration, in which he served, asserted the priority of economic rights in its foreign policy, in practice there was a concentration on political rights abroad:

> . . . Was this the right way to handle the problem? One way . . . is to say that if a nation cannot make its rhetoric consistent with its practice, then the best course is to change its rhetoric . . .
>
> I believe this view is mistaken for several reasons. First, it assumes that human rights are forever fixed and that the American contribution to the establishment of the fixed body of human rights was the definitive contribution . . . Second, this view reflects a very narrow reading of the history of this nation . . . our founding fathers were also determined to create a sufficient sense of community . . . that this country could survive. At times the pressure toward conformity in American life is painfully high. It is almost as though we all realize that we can philosophically tolerate creeds of extreme liberalism because we know of the

bracing pressures for conformity in this society. In effect, the founding fathers had two objectives: to control tyranny but to avoid the individualism and separation that could breed anarchy.

Maynes pointed out the dilemma of intended ends versus actual results in implementing human rights policy, as cited by critics of the Carter policies in the case of American policy towards Iran. He found that recent sensitivity to human rights internationally is derived from peoples, not governments, and is abetted by such modern communications means as the cassette recorder, the Xerox machine and the direct-dial telephone while the mass media enable more people everywhere to realize that all men and women belong to the same human family. For America's future human rights agenda, he proposed among other things that the United States foster the international sense of humanity, recognize that political and economic rights are interconnected, and encourage the development of local institutions to protect individual rights everywhere.

The Virginia Foundation for the Humanities and Public Policy, through a grant to the George Mason Project for the Study of Human Rights, made possible this second annual lecture series, "The Legacy of George Mason: The First Amendment," on which this volume is based. Members of the university community have been most helpful in the development of the lecture series and the publication of this work. Special mention should be made of the assistance of George W. Johnson, President; Martha Turnage, former Vice President for Public Affairs; Joan Fisher, former Vice President for Development; Robert T. Hawkes, Jr., Dean, Division of Continuing Education; Barbara Knight, Department of Public Affairs; Robert Davidow, School of Law; and Ruth Kerns, Fenwick Library. Richard B. O'Keeffe of Fenwick Library prepared the index. Special thanks also are due Professor A. E. Dick Howard, University of Virginia School of Law, for his wise counsel and many suggestions as our chief consultant since the Project's inception.

Finally, the vision and dediction which Josephine F. Pacheco of the George Mason University History Department has brought to the direction of this project is responsible for its initial and continuing success.

T. Daniel Shumate

George Mason University

Notes

1. Of the several studies of the Enlightenment in America the only one which devotes adequate attention to George Mason is Ernest Cassara, *The Enlightenment in America* (Boston: Twayne Publishers, 1975).

2. "The Library of John Mercer of Marlborough", compiled by Bennie Brown, Jr., October 6, 1981. Unpublished ms. Mr. Brown is Librarian at Gunston Hall Plantation, Lorton, Virginia.

3. Ralph Ketcham, *James Madison, A Biography* (New York: The Macmillan Company, 1971), 72–73. Mason had provided only for toleration by the state, not for "the free exercise of religion."

4. The successive drafts of the Virginia Declaration of Rights are printed and annotated with commentary in Robert A. Rutland, ed., *The Papers of George Mason, 1725–1792,* 3 vols. (Chapel Hill: The University of North Carolina Press, 1975), 1:274–291. This brief account of Mason at the Virginia Convention is based primarily on Rutland and on Helen Hill Miller, *George Mason, Gentleman Revolutionary* (Chapel Hill: The University of North Carolina Press, 1975), Chapter 7. The final draft of the Virginia Declaration is in the Appendix to this volume.

5. Sanford H. Cobb, *The Rise of Religious Liberty in America* (New York: Macmillan, 1902), 507–508. Texts of some of the new constitutions are printed in Richard L. Perry, ed., *Sources of our Liberties* (New York: McGraw Hill, 1959). See pp. 301–303 (Virginia); 323–357 (Pennsylvania, Maryland, North Carolina); 368–386 (Massachusetts, New Hampshire). Explanatory narratives precede each text.

6. Evarts B. Greene, *Religion and the State* (Ithaca, New York: Cornell University Press, 1941), 66.

7. See State constitution texts in Perry, *Sources of Our Liberties.*

8. J. J. Scarisbrick, *Henry VIII* (Berkeley: University of California Press, 1968), Chapter 9, is the basis for the summary of Henry's religious policy.

9. The remainder of this section to 1660 is based primarily on W. K. Jordan, *The Development of Religious Toleration in England,* 4 vols. (Gloucester, Massachusetts: Peter Smith, 1965). Vol. 1 covers developments in Queen Elizabeth's reign, Vol. 2 the reigns of James I and Charles I to 1640, and Vols. 3 and 4 the Puritan period from 1640 to 1660.

10. Sir George Clark, *The Later Stuarts, 1660–1714* (Oxford: At the Clarendon Press, 1955) is the reference source for political developments discussed in this period.

11. Lois G. Schwoerer, *The Declaration of Rights, 1689* (Baltimore: The Johns Hopkins University Press, 1981), 61–66.

12. Ibid., 58–62.

13. Basil Williams, *The Whig Supremacy, 1714–1760*, second ed. (Oxford: At the Clarendon Press, 1962) is the source for political developments in this period.

14. The account of the "Commonwealthmen" is drawn from Caroline Robbins, *The Eighteenth-Century Commonwealthman* (Cambridge, Massachusetts: Harvard University Press, 1959), passim.

15. Frederick S. Siebert, *Freedom of the Press in England, 1476–1776* (Urbana: University of Illinois Press, 1965). This section draws heavily on Siebert throughout and, where indicated, on Leonard Levy, *Legacy of Suppression: Freedom of Speech and Press in Early American History* (Cambridge, Massachusetts: The Belknap Press of Harvard University Press, 1964). Levy's chapters 3 and 4 cover the development of the theory of freedom of expression in England as well as America. Despite his controversial overall interpretation, his data are useful.

16. J. E. Neale, *Elizabeth I and her Parliaments,* 2 vols. (New York: St. Martin's Press, 1958), 2:156.

17. Siebert, *Freedom of the Press in England,* 201.

18. Ibid., 254. John Mercer's library included L'Estrange's *The Intelligencer* (London, 1663–1666).

19. Schwoerer, *The Declaration of Rights,* 108, 120.
20. Levy, *Legacy of Suppression,* 10.
21. Ibid., 145–148.
22. Ibid., 157–159.
23. Ibid., 149–157.
24. Siebert, *Freedom of the Press in England,* 385–392.
25. Sydney E. Ahlstrom, *A Religious History of the American People,* 2 vols. (New York: Image Books Division of Doubleday & Company, 1975). Volume I is the basis for much of the content of this section concerning all the colonies except Virginia.
26. The text of the Charter of Rhode Island and Providence Plantations of 1663 appears in Perry, *Sources of our Liberties,* 169–179.
27. Ibid., 166.
28. Ibid., 100.
29. Greene, *Religion and the State,* 66.
30. Carl Bridenbaugh, *Mitre & Sceptre* (New York: Oxford University Press, 1962) is the basis for the description of the effort to establish an episcopate in the colonies.
31. Ahlstrom, *A Religious History of the American People,* 1:454–456; Greene, *Religion and the State,* 67–69.
32. Perry, *Sources of Our Liberties,* 39–46, reproduces the text of the first Virginia Charter.
33. Greene, *Religion and the State,* 32; Cobb, *The Rise of Religious Liberty in America,* is the source for most of the data in this section concerning colonial Virginia before 1740. After that date the major source is Rhys Isaac, *The Transformation of Virginia, 1740–1790* (Chapel Hill: The University of North Carolina Press, 1982).
34. Cobb, *The Rise of Religious Liberty in America,* 91–92.
35. Rutland, *Papers of George Mason,* 1:4–5, 28–30.
36. Isaac, *The Transformation of Virginia,* devotes Chapter 8 to this topic.
37. Cobb, *The Rise of Religious Liberty in America,* 103–104.
38. Ibid., 108–111. Helen Hill Miller, *The Case for Liberty* (Chapel Hill: The University of North Carolina Press, 1965) discusses Separate Baptist agitation and the "Parson's Cause" in Chapter 1.
39. Robert Douthat Meade, *Patrick Henry,* 2 vols. (Philadelphia: J. B. Lippincott Company, 1957–1969). Vol. 1, Chapter 8 is devoted to the "Parson's Cause."

40. Isaac, *The Transformation of Virginia*, 182–189.

41. Ketcham, *James Madison, A Biography*, 58.

42. Levy, *Legacy of Suppression*, is the basis for this section unless otherwise indicated.

43. Ibid., 21–22.

44. Ibid., 24–30.

45. Arthur E. Schlesinger, *Prelude to Independence* (New York: Knopf, 1958), Chapter 1. Robert M. Weir, "The Role of the Newspaper Press in the Southern Colonies on the Eve of the Revolution: An Interpretation," in Bernard Bailyn and John B. Hench, eds., *The Press & The American Revolution* (Worcester, Massachusetts: American Antiquarian Society, 1980), 99–150.

46. Levy, *Legacy of Suppression*, 36–38.

47. Miller, *The Case for Liberty*, devotes Chapter 2 to the Zenger trial.

48. The Pennsylvania background of Hamilton is discussed in Levy, *Legacy of Suppression*, 51–52.

49. The importance of James Alexander in the development of the theory of a free press is discussed by Levy, 133–137.

50. The remainder of this section is based primarily on Schlesinger, *Prelude to Independence*.

51. Stephen Botein, "Printers and the American Revolution," Bailyn and Hench, *The Press & the American Revolution*, 40–42, 72–73.

52. Weir, "The Newspaper Press in the Southern Colonies," 109–110.

53. "To the Committee of Merchants in London," June 6, 1766, Rutland, *Papers of George Mason*, 1:65–72.

54. Botein, "Printers and the American Revolution," 42–45.

55. Isaac, *The Transformation of Virginia*, Chapter 12 and Thomas E. Buckley, *Church and State in Revolutionary Virginia, 1776–1787* (Charlottesville: University Press of Virginia, 1977) are the basis for this section except as otherwise indicated.

56. "Amendment to the Bill Exempting Dissenters from Contributing to the Established Church," Dec. 5, 1776, Rutland, *Papers of George Mason*, 1:318–319.

57. Rutland, *Papers of George Mason*, 2:834–835, summarizes Mason's actions concerning Madison's Remonstrance.

58. Robert A. Rutland, *The Birth of the Bill of Rights, 1776–*

1791, revised edition (Boston: Northeastern University Press, 1983), 100–101; Perry, *Sources of Our Liberties*, 387–391. The text of the Ordinance is in Perry on 392–397.

59. "Fairfax County Freeholders' Address and Instructions to Their General Assembly Delegates," May 30, 1783, Rutland, *Papers of George Mason*, 2:779–782.

60. Miller, *George Mason, Gentleman Revolutionary*, Chapter 12 is the basis for the accounts of the Mount Vernon Conference and the Annapolis Convention.

61. Ibid., Chapters 12 and 13, are the source of personal detail concerning Mason and the Philadelphia Convention. The account of the convention proceedings is based on Rutland, *Birth of the Bill of Rights*, Chapter 6. Excerpts from Madison's and others' journals concerning Mason's participation at Philadelphia are reprinted in Rutland, *Papers of George Mason*, 3:885–991.

62. Mason's objections are printed in Rutland, *Papers of George Mason*, 3:991–994.

63. Miller, *George Mason, Gentleman Revolutionary*, 268.

64. The ratification narrative in other colonies is based on Rutland, *Birth of the Bill of Rights*, Chapter 8, and in Virginia on both Rutland and on Miller, *George Mason, Gentleman Revolutionary*, Chapter 15, except as noted.

65. The statistics are from a table in Edward Dumbauld, *The Bill of Rights and What It Means Today* (Norman: University of Oklahoma Press, 1957), 161.

66. Robert Douthat Meade, *Patrick Henry*, 2:347–348.

67. The fight for the passage of Madison's proposed amendments in Congress is drawn from Rutland, *Birth of the Bill of Rights*, Chapter 9, and Irving Brant, *The Bill of Rights: Its Origin and Meaning* (New York: New American Library, Inc., 1975), Chapter 4.

68. Dumbauld, *The Bill of Rights and What It Means Today*, reproduces in Appendices all the amendments proposed by the states and the successive drafts in Congress of the Bill of Rights.

69. Mason to Samuel Griffin, September 8, 1791, Rutland, *Papers of George Mason*, 3:1172.

70. The ratification narrative is based on Rutland, *Birth of the Bill of Rights*, Chapter 9, and Levy, *Legacy of Suppression*, 221–233.

71. Miller, *George Mason, Gentleman Revolutionary*, Chapter 16, contains a fine overview of Mason's impact on Europe.

1

George Mason and the Origins of the First Amendment

ROBERT RUTLAND
Professor of History
University of Virginia

The emotions released by the Revolution left many Americans deeply dedicated to the aim of keeping in being a society whose members, whatever their differences in wealth, education, fortune, or social style, would respect one another as equals. The force of this feeling was easy to sense but not easy to fix.
—J. R. Pole, *The Pursuit of Equality in American History*

RESPECT FOR THE LAW AND EQUALITY UNDER THE LAW HAVE BEEN great themes in American history. Indeed, such was the respect of our Founding Fathers for law that, in order to overthrow British rule, they first had to invoke the natural law that allows rebellion in a tyranny and then take all the precedents they could find from the English revolutions of 1641 and 1688 to give their activities the stamp of historical authenticity. The self-evident truth "that all men are born equally free and independent, and have certain inherent natural rights," which George Mason used as his ringing opener for the Virginia Declaration of Rights, epitomized this respect for law in a time of some disorder. Life and liberty, property and happiness, none of these could be held dear if there was no law, and the law was a mockery without the basic assumption that all stood equal before every magistrate.

We need to remind ourselves of these underpinnings to the movement known to history as the American Revolution. As Professor Lawrence Stone pointed out in another context, these ideas were "a time bomb" brought forward from earlier English experience, expanded by the American one, and they exploded with such force that they still exist as the fundamental reason why there is a cleavage or iron curtain or whatever you wish to call it between eastern Europe and western civilization. Much of the constitutional law since our Civil War has to do with striking a balance between equality and liberty, and we must remind ourselves that less than three decades ago millions of American citizens were still sitting in the rear of buses and drinking at separate fountains for blacks and whites. What has happened since 1954 in education, housing, public facilities, and the everyday traffic patterns of life is certainly proof that this is still a government of laws and not of men—that America is a law-abiding nation—and that the deepest sources of our political existence relate to the Bill of Rights as it has come to be interpreted in our time.

This is not to say, however, that George Mason had a vision of civil liberty or individual rights very much like what we have today. There is a good chance that George Mason would be aghast at some of the constitutional developments of the last century; but if we think of the libertarian bias that dominated his thinking it becomes fairly clear that Mason had a flexibility of mind remarkable for his day, deserving both our respect and our imitation. During the 18th century men were whipped and hung, their ears were cut off and their thumbs branded, and in Mason's time that kind of punishment was accepted—at least it was swift and carried a certain amount of efficiency into the crime-deterring process. These extreme examples appall us today, but let it be remembered that there were safeguards in Mason's Declaration of Rights so that accused persons could not be found guilty without due process of law. Some of our citizens may be a bit alarmed at the lengths to which we have gone in defining "due process," but it is our national glory that we have never had a quartering rack or torture chamber in this country. As long as we have our Constitution and Bill of Rights, we never will.

Beyond the gains of this century embodied in the Fourth and Fifth Amendments we still find ourselves wondering about the limits of freedom defined in the First Amendment. In this paper I want to suggest that George Mason and the other Founding Fathers valued the First Amendment for reasons far removed from its present-day interpretation. To be explicit, I believe there are good grounds for saying that George Mason and his fellow Virginian James Madison thought the purpose of the First Amendment was to preserve our political—not our personal—freedom. The rights we associate with religious freedom, freedom of the press, freedom of speech, the right to assembly, and the right to petition our elected representatives were not considered to be what we call today "civil liberties." More on this later. The topic is timely since attention is being focused on our constitutional history as the bicentennial year looms and the ideas propounded by our Founding Fathers—most particularly by Jefferson but also to some extent Madison, Hamilton, and the master of Gunston Hall—are attracting scholarly attention.

This revival of interest in the mental apparatus of our Founding Fathers is in itself instructive. It seems that every time our nation goes on a conservative binge, so to speak, and turns the helm over to national leaders who are elected for their pragmatism, no-nonsense approach, and businesslike attitude in the White House the academic community reacts by producing a counterbalance of rhetoric dealing with our national origins. To mention only a couple of examples, works that come to mind as having erupted from periods noted for their intellectual placidity or normality are Vernon L. Parrington's three books lumped together as *Main Currents in American Thought* from the Coolidge era and Louis Hartz's *Liberal Tradition in America* from the Eisenhower years. No doubt the Reagan era will produce its own equivalents of these landmarks, proving that Newton's Third Law applies in history as well as physics. I hope we never tire of talking about the origins of our political freedom, about where we found this precious liberty that so sharply delineates the major political philosophies in the 20th century.

Despite our day-to-day concern for balanced budgets, trips in space, and nuclear parity, the fact remains that the signal event in American history was and still is the American Revolution. In a sense, the nation never recovered from its impact. Our perceptions of international politics and economics, of the Third World, and of our involvement in Latin America are all sharpened when we think of the American Revolution as one of the major turning points in the history of western civilization.[1] Without that in mind, much of world history since 1776 does not make a great deal of sense. Robert R. Palmer's marvelous work, *The Age of the Democratic Revolution,* makes this point and it cannot be overstressed. For the American Revolution exalted *mankind.* Until the American and French Revolutions, most men lived short lives and hoped (or said they hoped) to be rewarded in the hereafter. As the ideas from 1775 went up like a mushroom cloud, drifting over the earth, the intellectual fallout affected men's minds profoundly. A new vision of a paradise on earth seemed feasible. Some deep chord in the human soul was struck by the notion that life and liberty and the pursuit of happiness are worthwhile goals, deserving the sacrifice of all the blood and treasure demanded.

One has to be aware of the threads of consistency that hold together much of the revolutionary fabric. Take Jefferson, going from the authorship of *A Summary View of the Rights of British America*, on to the Continental Congress and the Declaration of Independence, and then to become secretary of state and president. Or take Washington's departure from the Continental Congress for Boston in 1775 and all that took place until he finally returned to Mount Vernon permanently in 1797. Or look at Madison, starting at the Virginia Convention in 1776 at twenty-five and moving in the highest echelons of leadership until he retired to Montpelier in 1817. Indeed, Mason is almost an exception for (as we know) he could have picked his own place in the councils of the nation but chose instead to go out on sorties, usually within the Old Dominion, make his contribution, and then escape the heat of battle or debate by retreating to Gunston Hall. But why the consistency, and why the concentration of such talent in Virginia?

The explanation has to come from the circumstances that culminated in the whole sweep of American history after 1765. Although we like to think of this as a strictly American movement, it was not. There was a distinctiveness about the American tilt of the Enlightenment, but the intellectual movement had been filtered through Europe, and the historical roots were English. The nomenclature of the Revolution, with its "conventions," committees of safety, and even its declaration of rights, was borrowed from the English experience between 1640 and 1689. With the single exception of avoiding any pretense of wanting a king, the Americans of 1775 looked upon themselves as the descendants—spiritual if not genealogical—of the Englishmen who in short order destroyed the idea of divine right for kings and instead talked at great length about "the people."

"The people" were the men who paid the taxes, made the laws, enforced the laws, held the property, and saw their rising prosperity threatened by archaic methods and customs that allowed one man or a few men at best to make the critical decisions in the nation. So the English produced their Cromwell, chopped off a monarch's head, and then went back to a constitutional monarchy enveloped in a new set of rules, customs, and laws that made much of England's earlier political system as anachronistic as an ice cream social in the Kennedy Center.[2]

This wave of modern thought, developed in England by Queen Anne's time, provided the revolutionary antecedents of American events in the 1760s and 1770s. Old grievances led to new rights—all subsumed under the general term: Liberty. What did "Liberty" mean? Liberty represented, among other things, a novel way of thinking about life. Old institutions and traditions remained in force at a time when men went through the forms of a life that made little sense. The findings of Newton, Copernicus, and lesser intellects led to a refreshing vision of what life could be like on earth—and although it took centuries for this scientific revolution to have its total impact (indeed, we are only now coming to realize its full implications), the immutable facts of nature were translated into new forms of government and gave a broad, different philosophical basis to life itself. Consider—had Jefferson lived in 13th-century Europe he might have risen to be a cardinal, but that distance of five centuries was the broadest of gulfs, and one result was that Jefferson and most of the Virginians of his day *never* considered a career in either the church or the army. The new liberty involved secular career choices that had no roots in the old feudal order. In fact, as the

Enlightenment movement spread, those old avenues of social mobility made no sense in America. The humanitarianism of the Virginia gentry was probably the finest expression of the Enlightenment in America between 1775 and 1791, and it came from men nurtured in a plantation economy. To a man Mason, Madison, Jefferson, and Washington were the products of a system that exalted human reason, virtue, and justice. Unlike political leaders in our skeptical age, the Virginians who were gentlemen freeholders believed that "a new age is dawning." A sense of duty called upon them to make the new nation the finest expression of all the Enlightenment represented.

The impact of the humanistic Enlightenment thinking was imperceptible at first. Perhaps it really began after Henry VIII tore up the roots of the mother church in England. By the time James II had alienated most of his subjects there was a definite and strong hint of more change in the air. Our Jamestown, the Virginia port named to honor James I, is now a famous ghost town. James II and his way of thinking symbolized the death rattle of the old order. The Englishmen who came to America in the generations just before and after James abdicated were infected with a virus that we call by a variety of names—enterprise, greed, or ambition—but which boiled down to immense drive and a practical sense of getting on in the world. Yes, in the *world.* The established church that had been so powerful in Europe, and held a large measure of power in protestant England, was a weak reed in Virginia almost from the start.

Of course churches were built and ministers sermonized, but there was a world of difference between the theocrats of New England and the dedicated Virginia-born Americans of English descent. The seeds of humanistic Enlightenment thought—which in one sense went far beyond formal religion—took root as Bacon's Rebellion was stamped out. The excesses of cruelty gave way to a more humane way of living. No wonder that Beccarria was read in Virginia, and we can imagine the cringing that took place when the corpses of felons were allowed to rot on the gallows. The stench of that decaying flesh and of the hands and thumbs and ears scorched by red-hot brands applied to fulfill a court order left their mark on men's minds.

Yet this was the Virginia of George Mason, and to some degree Mason straddled the old era of propriety and the new age of reform. He could approve the cutting off of a runaway slave's ear, but he also went along with suggestions that cruel and unusual punishment had no place in modern society. Obviously, to Mason there was a vast difference between a quick stroke of a sharp razor and torture chambers. Let us remember too that Mason's contemporary, Dr. Guillotin, devised his instrument of execution in the name of humanity.[3]

Could Mason be an enlightened humanist and a vestryman at Truro Parish at the same time? I think nearly all of the Virginia galaxy that included Madison, Jefferson, Mason, Washington, and a few others were respectful and proper when in the vicinity of their parish meetinghouses. But I cannot see them searching for guidance in their day-to-day affairs from Bible passages. We know they held horse races on Sunday afternoons and argued with ministers over salaries and allowed churches to fall into disrepair at an alarming rate. Why was this? I suggest it was owing to a fundamental shift in thinking that left organized formal religion outside the mainstream of Virginia life. By Mason's time the old shopworn arguments concerning Biblical texts and meanings had grown tedious in plantation society. Conversation had shifted to worldly matters—land prices, tobacco crops, road and harbor building, and other practical affairs. If Virginians kept up the appearance of attachment to old, formal religious ties, it was often simply as a means of keeping control of local tax or tithe rates and for "going along" with a system of local government that was nominally related to the parishes, but secular in inspiration and execution.

To be sure, when tensions mounted after 1764 and days of fasting and prayer were called for, the purpose was to crystallize public opinion on behalf of resistance. With the postulate that resistance to tyrants was obedience to God, all one needed was the vulnerable tyrant. Conveniently, George III fitted that unlikely role after a decade that began with Mason declaring himself "firmly attached to the present royal Family upon the Throne, unalienably affected to his Majesty's sacred Person & Government, in the Defence of which he wou'd shed the last Drop of his Blood" and closed with Mason serving on the committee of safety pledged to American independence.[4] What did he have to lose? Everything. Gunston Hall, his family estate, his honor, and his place in society that predetermined his revolutionary role. The risks Mason and his generation ran were enormous. But they believed they were forced by history into their roles and that they were only walking in the footsteps other Englishmen had trod in the seventeenth century. In the midst of the Revolution Mason remarked that "taking a retrospective view of what is passed, we seem to have been treading upon enchanted Ground."[5] That was his way of saying that the risks forced him to decide whether to stand for his king or his country—and the great Virginians stood by their country. No ambiguity, no soul-search, but only a clear belief that they were right and England was wrong. (Oh blessed polarization: We will never see its like again!)

So Mason and his friends struggled to keep the distant hand of Parliament out of their affairs. Failing there, they fell back to embargoes, fasting, prayers, and finally to muskets, artillery, and sabers. And all of this came while invoking the cause of a freeborn Englishman's rights.

If Mason was impatient with the ministry in England, he was hardly less at ease with some of his fellow Virginians in the resistance movement. When he took Washington's place in the 1775 Virginia Convention, Mason told his neighbor he had never been "in so disagreeable a Situation, and almost despaired of a Cause which I saw so ill conducted. . . . However after some Weeks, the Bablers were pretty well silenced, a few weighty Members began to take the Lead, several whol[e]some Regulations were made, and if the Convention had continued to sit a few Days longer, I think the public Safety wou'd have been as well provided for as our present Circumstances permit."[6] Short of temper, Mason was long in confidence. By the next spring he and like-minded Virginians knew what had to be done: sever the last tie with England. There Mason played perhaps the major role of his political life—coming to Williamsburg a few days late, perceiving the tenor of the Convention of 1776, and cutting through the committee red tape by writing a declaration of rights almost single-handedly.

We cannot overstress the fact that Mason's draft of the Virginia Declaration of Rights is the grandfather of *all* the bills of rights. Not only is it one of the great state papers of the American Revolution, it is a milestone in the development of the worldwide Enlightenment. Henceforth, "the Enjoyment of Life and Liberty, with the Means of acquiring and possessing Property, and pursueing and obtaining Happiness and Safety" has been a beacon light for mankind. It is our best product—our best export—far more efficient than our missiles and rockets and our "military advisers" that we seem to rely upon these days.

At the time, Mason's draft went beyond the abstractions to bring forward practical results for the revolution. Not only was a philosophy of government with a separation of powers made distinct; there was a curtailment of the powers that governments might exercise. An accused person should be granted a speedy trial in the vicinity of the alleged crime and could not be called upon to give testimony that could incriminate him. Bills of attainder and ex post facto laws were denounced as "dangerous, and ought to be avoided." Religion was to be "governed only by Reason and Conviction, not by Force or Violence; and therefore . . . all Men shou'd enjoy the fullest Toleration in the Exercise of Religion, according to the Dictates of Conscience."[7] At Madison's suggestion, that provision was expanded to an unqualified freedom of conscience; and freedom of the press, "being the great bulwark of Liberty," was hailed as an indispensable ingredient of a free government. Much of it sounds familiar—all of it sounds good. Within days, the message was moving in all directions. By 1789, the brightest men in Europe were hailing Mason's draft and its final form as a clarion call to humankind on every continent.

There seems to have been little argument about the provisions in Mason's declaration of rights. The delegates in Williamsburg had read their volumes of John Locke, Algernon Sydney, and other commentators from an earlier era of revolution. But how could slaveholders talk of freedom and liberty? This is something that may disturb us until we realize that Mason and his generation were accustomed to thinking of the white man's social order as a society they had been born into and which could only be changed gradually. We know they talked about slavery in Williamsburg that summer, but there seems to have been a common agreement that the first problem to be conquered was the British ministry's will to wage war.[8] In time, Mason was to condemn slavery in the most bitter terms, but in 1776 the practical matter of replacing the royal government with a working state system based on republican principles was the first priority. We know how rapidly the other colonies working on state constitutions picked up the Virginia declaration and incorporated its provisions into their codes. By 1778, Mason's influence was seen in the fundamental laws enacted from North Carolina to New Hampshire.

His reputation in Virginia was now firm. He had to beg off service in the Continental Congress and could have chosen any office in the commonwealth by a nod of the head. His propensity to avoid the limelight is well known, but even though Mason preferred "the happiness of independance & a private Station to the troubles and Vexations of Public Business," he bestirred himself whenever a great issue was involved. Thus, when a seeming conflict with Article 16 in the Virginia Declaration of Rights (freedom of conscience) came before the state legislature in 1785, Mason worked with Madison to circulate the *Memorial & Remonstrance* that was the beginning of the end of the established church in Virginia. Madison quoted Article 16 and wrote: "If we recur to its origin, it is equally the gift of nature; if we weigh its importance, it cannot be less dear to us." In the state declaration of rights, the matter of a free conscience held "studied emphasis," Madison said, and if the legislature could invade the field of religion "they may sweep away all our fundamental rights."[9] Mason needed little urging as he broadcast printed copies of Madison's argument, circulating it as a petition to be signed and sent to the 1786 session of the General Assembly. Proponents of a subsidy for Christian churches lost their battle, opening a gap which Madison soon exploited by introducing Jefferson's bill establishing religious freedom in the most unequivocal terms. A few years later, Madison introduced the bill of rights in Congress. By 1791 it was the supreme law of the land. Mason was pleased.

In the life of every public man there are inconsistencies, but in Mason's case he came down so hard and so right on religion that we can say he was steadfastly consistent in insisting upon that initial clause of the First Amendment. If someday we find that Mason's personal library contained *Cato's Letters*, that handbook of the revolutionary generation, I hope a particular page will have one section underlined by Mason's pen:

> Without Freedom of Thought, there can be no such Thing as Wisdom; and no such Thing as publick Liberty, without Freedom of Speech; which is the Right of every Man, as far as by it he does not hurt or controul the Right of another. . . . This sacred Privilege is so essential to free Governments, that the Security of Property and the Freedom of Speech always go together; and in those wretched Countries where a Man cannot call his Tongue his own, he can scarce call any Thing else his own.[10]

For Mason's commitment from 1776 onward was for freedom of the mind. And in all ages and all times, men who labor on behalf of liberty of conscience and speech gain heroic stature.

In Mason's case, his heroism rose from his role as an agent for change. The reason Mason's statue is on the Capitol grounds in Richmond is that in his grasp of revolutionary statecraft he constantly sought to give meaning to the words "liberty" and "freedom." But let me suggest that in the context of Enlightenment thinking, Mason believed that the best way to assure the sacred rights of "generations unborn" was to limit the powers of government. So I come to the point of asking whether the freedom Mason spoke of was personal, or was that liberty to be achieved by limitations on governmental power? In short, does the First Amendment protect free speech or freedom of religion so that a zealous citizen may spout obscenities in public with impunity, or was the First Amendment conceived as a means of preserving a republican form of government? I think Mason was thinking of the latter and nothing more.

The Supreme Court decides, but no one suggests the highest court has a corner on infallibility. Many citizens have honest doubts concerning rulings on actions in the fields of pornography, school prayers, penal incarceration, abortions, and capital punishment. Certainly there is no proof that the changed judicial attitudes prevailing since World War II have made us a freer society. Which is more humane—to give a wrongdoer forty lashes and let him go, or to throw him into a prison and keep him there three years? Is it better to hold a speedy trial in the vicinage of a criminal act or to allow a capricious change of venue and then go through an appeal process that might take five or six years, at a cost to society of several hundred thousand dollars? In our time, we have seen the First Amendment used to shield flagburners and those strange citizens who want to be called the American Nazi party. This has brought the court into a kind of confrontation with what has come to be known as the Establishment.

In Mason's time, he was part of the Establishment. Mason probably disliked unruly mobs as much as Washington, but he was not shocked by the Boston Tea Party, and he approved the intimidating process that sent his kinsman scurrying back to London instead of settling in as the stamp distributor in Virginia. From 1765 onward change was definitely in the air in the thirteen colonies. The result was that a group of once-dependent colonies set themselves up as a republic. The purpose of that republic was to give its citizens the blessings of liberty. The question then as now was: how do restrictions on individual freedoms jeopardize the blessings of liberty?

For our answer, let us look at the First Amendment. After the committees finished their work, it contained only forty-five words. Ratified by December 1791, the amendment was unused for generation after generation. To the contemporaries of Mason and Madison, the purpose of the amendment was to preserve republican institutions by preventing governmental interference in the specified areas of religion, press, assembly, and petition. As to religion, an important direct antecedent of the amendment was the dialogue in Orange County, Virginia, where Madison had to deal with the Baptists at election time. Elder John Leland, asked to spell out his objections to the proposed constitution in 1788, followed Mason's lead in his introduction—"There is no Bill of Rights"—and saved his strongest argument for the last point. "What is clearest of all—*Religious Liberty,* is not Sufficiently Secured, No Religious test is Required as a Qualification to fill any office under the United States, but if a Majority of Congress with the President favor one System more than another, they may oblige all others to pay to the Support of their System as much as they please . . . & if the Manners of the People are so far Corrupted, that they cannot live by Republican principles, it is Very *Dangerous leaving* Religious Liberty at their Mercy."[11] This statement was aimed directly at Madison, and he measured its importance. The whole point was that Baptists feared some kind of a national church might be established by law—it was not a fear that they would be individually harassed or persecuted. They knew that day was past. Religious liberty clearly meant one thing only: NO state church.

Or take abridging the freedom of the press. Although the First Amendment forbids Congress to pass any law touching on freedom of the press, Congress soon passed one that put a clamp on the opposition press—the Sedition Act of 1798—and that law was rigorously applied by sitting justices of the Supreme Court who never doubted that they were doing the right thing. Editors were hounded, thrown in jail, fined, and in some cases their health was wrecked—and the cases never went on appeal to the Supreme Court.[12]

Why not? For one thing, *all* the branches of the federal government were united, temporarily, in suppressing what they considered the danger represented by Jefferson's Republican party—and any time those branches that are supposed to be balancing and checking each other's power are working in concert, then the progress of democratic government is stopped. That was the case in 1799, and it took the election of 1800 to get the country moving in a democratic direction again.

Moreover, although Jefferson granted pardons and remitted fees to undo the damage of the Sedition Act, he never viewed the First Amendment as a means of protecting individual printers and editors whose newspapers attacked the administration with scurrilous innuendos, filling columns with remarks about the "anti-Christ" in the White House or the Frenchified Republican party. As Leonard Levy reminded us, Jefferson thought a few well-directed prosecutions of Federalist editors might have a salutary effect, and he was pleased when one Harry Crosswell was taken into court, charged with "seditiously libeling the President."[13] Crosswell was a third-rate newspaperman running a fourth-rate paper, the Hudson *Wasp*, but his barbs got under Jefferson's skin. Crosswell was indicted under the common law, Alexander Hamilton sprang to Crosswell's defense, and before long there was talk of bringing Jefferson to New York to testify. Jefferson never went north of Bethesda, of course, and Crosswell was found guilty; but Hamilton had made a point of saying that truth ought to be admitted as a defense in a prosecution against an editor. Jefferson backed off and in time gave up his efforts to teach editors lessons. But my point is that even Jefferson saw the First Amendment as unrelated to the personal rights of a newspaperman who drew a fine line between libel and fair comment.

Let us remember that in the first decade or so after 1791 most of Mason's revolutionary cronies—Jefferson certainly and James Madison—saw that many of their assumptions about the efficacy of the First Amendment as well as most of the rest of the Bill of Rights had proved incorrect. In 1791 Madison had argued that once the Bill of Rights was part of the Constitution "independent tribunals of justice will consider themselves in a peculiar manner the guardians of those rights." Armed with the several amendments, Madison had then argued, the courts would provide "an impenetrable bulwark against every assumption of power in the legislative or executive" branches and "be naturally led to resist every encroachment upon rights expressly stipulated for in the constitution by the declaration of rights."[14]

While Mason was still alive and listening for assurances, Madison had spoken in Congress of the underlying presumption of the day, that the state legislatures were "the sure guardians of the people's liberty."[15] Indeed, Madison had written a separate amendment for a bill of rights that would have specifically applied all the provisions to the states, but that plan had been rejected in 1791. Thus the Bill of Rights was looked upon in 1791, and again in *Barron* v. *Baltimore* in 1819, as a check upon Congress and the federal government and not upon the states. And in 1845 the Supreme Court again said that the First Amendment "makes no provision for protecting the citizens of the respective states in their religious liberties; this is left to the state constitutions and laws."[16] Repeatedly the high court took that view until the log jam began to break in 1925 with the Gitlow case, and—of course—the dam broke in the Near case of 1931 when the court said that a Minnesota law gagging the press was "an infringement of the liberty of the press guaranteed by the Fourteenth."[17] That decision was the shoehorn case—all of the civil rights we think of now as protected by the courts were slipped in under the same general rule that involves the due process of law and the equal protection of the laws as set forth in the Fourteenth Amendment. Without that Fourteenth

Amendment umbrella, Dan Rather and Roger Mudd would have to be far more careful, and the *National Enquirer* would now be in bankruptcy.

Well, not quite. But we all know that the tremendous gains in the field of civil rights, stretching from that Near decision to *Brown* v. *Board of Education* and on to our day, have come through an expanded view of what the Constitution means in terms of personal liberties. And I must say that while I applaud our broadened sense of personal freedom, we have forgotten the original purposes of the First Amendment. And that takes us back to George Mason.

I said earlier Mason was an agent for change. But that agency was on behalf of a general principle—not for the sake of a religious zealot's right to sell flowers in an airport or for an editor to have the right to defame a politician with impunity. Mason and Madison were the only plantation owners who dabbled in constitution-making—poking around where lawyers usually did the writing—and probably we can say that their influence was extraordinary because their constitutions and bills of rights were succinct, to the point, and even the average man read them and understood them.

The American of their day was indeed a free man. He was lightly taxed, he could move anywhere he wanted to move, and he could go to church or not go to church as the mood moved him. If he ran his farm or plantation efficiently, he hardly had time to read newspapers or books, he was always working or eating or drinking or sleeping. But he was a free man. Once a year he could vote or he could stay in the field and let others vote. Most of the time he didn't bother to vote at all—my recollection is that fewer than five percent of the eligible voters in Virginia actually voted for Madison in 1812—but the important point is that the Virginian in 1791 and 1812 believed himself to be a free man. Why was he free?

Because he lived under a republican form of government, with elected representatives whose duty it was to maintain the republic and guarantee to every white citizen life, liberty, and the pursuit of happiness. This was not a complicated program.

The clamor over the Bill of Rights that Mason evoked with his 1787 pamphlet, *Objections to This Constitution of Government,* struck a chord because of the general fear of authority. Although the American was not expecting to run afoul of the authorities unless he spoke his piece too loudly or failed to pay his taxes—he still wanted it written down as his right to be left alone, as long as he obeyed the laws. Thus when the Constitution of 1787 was sent out, with Washington's endorsing letter displayed so prominently, it took a lot of courage for Mason to refuse to sign the Constitution. But Mason never courted popularity, and as we know his ringing first sentence in that pamphlet, "There is no Declaration of Rights," was paraphrased by preacher Leland and came to haunt the Federalists. Finally the Federalists had to back down and promise to add a bill of rights to the Constitution. Madison kept that promise, for politicians in those days took their promises seriously. Two years after his pamphlet attack, Mason told an old friend the amendments sent to the states for ratification pleased him and that a couple dealing with the judiciary and commercial laws would gratify him even more. Then, he said, "I cou'd chearfully put my Hand & Heart to the New Government."[18]

Notice that Mason did not ask for more amendments dealing with personal liberties. He obviously was satisfied with the suggested amendments Madison had submitted after his sifting through the long lists proposed at the several ratifying conventions. In his last years, Mason was comfortable with the way human rights were protected in this new republic—

he was uncomfortable about the means afforded to planters to make their living in a country more and more dominated by bankers and shippers.

As for the First Amendment, which now gave Mason peace of mind, it was, as we have seen, to remain a dormant amendment for generations insofar as the courts were concerned, but it was in one sense always a hard-working amendment because it embodied the political rights of the nation. The main purpose of the First Amendment as ratified in 1791 was to keep the republic alive. To ensure the success of the republican experiment the press was free to criticize the course of government and provide for peaceable transitions—it gave newspapers the immunity necessary to work without censorship and thus carry on the "censure of public officers and [make] charges of official misconduct."[19] In the same way, Congress was prevented from tampering with religion because all of the Founding Fathers, and perhaps none more than Mason, feared that a state church might be established. Mason's promotion of Madison's *Memorial & Remonstrance* is sufficient proof of his credentials on separation of church and state. That clause in the First Amendment was meant to prevent anything like a national church developing in this country and was one of the most important decisions made during the revolutionary era, sparing this nation from the spectacles of bloodshed, bigotry, and intolerance that still plague mankind and grab headlines every week. In 1749 Benjamin Franklin had said: "*History* will . . . afford frequent Opportunities of showing the Necessity of a *Publick Religion*, from its Usefulness to the Publick; the Advantage of a Religious Character among private Persons; the Mischiefs of Superstition, &c. and the Excellency of the CHRISTIAN RELIGION above all others antient or modern."[20] Just twenty-seven years later Mason, the Truro Parish vestryman, saw that freedom of conscience was not a matter for state concern. An enlightened Franklin was bound to agree.

As for the other First Amendment rights—peaceable assembly and petition—who can doubt that they too were not viewed as personal rights but were considered as part of a broad scheme to ensure public discussion and to keep representatives in touch with the people who elected them? Town meetings and vestry meetings were a part of the vital political processes of the day, providing community leaders with a forum while offering freeholders and parishioners a chance to speak their minds. An old hand at writing petitions, Mason believed that this simple device afforded every citizen a means of communicating with the elected assemblies. The art of petitioning is now pretty much lost, but in Mason's day it was a valued resource and important method of expressing views that lawmakers might ignore only at their peril. The Fairfax Resolves, which sounded the alarm bell of the American Revolution, came from a public meeting in Alexandria and were written as a petition to the Virginia Convention of 1774. If Parliament had listened, the whole course of history would have been different. But Parliament would not listen. The fundamental right of petition had been disparaged.

So the whole point of the First Amendment was reflective of George Mason's experience as a participant in the American Revolution and an expression of the manner in which the happy outcome of that revolution could be preserved. Other amendments took care of trial by jury, self-incrimination, cruel and unusual punishment, and other protections meant to serve individual citizens. But in my view the First Amendment was shaped to protect the republic from its domestic enemies who might attempt to shut off all public discussion, shackle the nation with an established church, and deny the people access to their elected representatives.

It would be fruitless to attempt to unravel all the First Amendment decisions in our courts since 1931—the Constitution is after all a "living document" and the world of 1791 is not our world in 1983. On the other hand, a great many frivolous lawsuits could be avoided if the historic antecedents of the First Amendment received more attention from our court system. A vast burden could be lifted from the courts by a refusal to make the First Amendment a constitutional grab bag.

George Mason and his generation shocked the world by their pronouncements on the rights of humankind to life and liberty. Their constitution-making had shattered the old myth of divine right—*vox populi, vox dei*—and proved that men were capable of handling their own affairs in an enlightened way. We have no conception of what a fresh breeze moved west to east, exciting the best minds in England and Europe, foretelling wave after wave of immigrants who would soon move toward this republic where liberty was stamped on every coin and on every heart.

"The striking Example of our happy country does I can assure you contribute more strongly to keep alive the hopes and Exertions of the friends of Liberty [here] than any thing else," American Minister Charles Pinckney wrote from Amsterdam in 1801. "Notwithstanding all their Errors & mistakes, their best informed men are confident that something like our constitution will one day issue from their Exertions & this animates & renders them easy under all their Burthens."[21]

Europeans still groaned under their burdens of conscription, war, famine, and oppression. America was at peace, and her people were well-fed and free. A strong republic would guard their personal rights, but first the republic itself had to be guarded. That was the function of the First Amendment and part of the enduring legacy from George Mason's generation. How fortunate that he lived when he did and where he did. What better trustee for "generations unborn?"

Notes

1. I say this despite A. L. Rowse's warning that "we historians are . . . too generous in our estimate of the importance of revolutions. . . . Yet I wonder whether there are not quieter, underlying movements . . . which are more fundamental and achieve more durable results in the history of mankind" ("Tudor Expansion: The Transition from Medieval to Modern History," *William and Mary Quarterly*, 3d ser., 14 [1957]: 309–10).

2. Caroline Robbins, "Rights and Grievances at Carpenters' Hall, 5 September–26 October 1774," *Pennsylvania History*, 43 (1976): 101–18.

3. R. R. Palmer, *The Age of the Democratic Revolution*, 2 vols. (Princeton: Princeton University Press, 1959–64), 2:22.

4. "To the Committee of Merchants in London," 6 June 1766, R. A. Rutland, ed., *The Papers of George Mason*, 3 vols. (Chapel Hill: The University of North Carolina Press, 1970), 1:71.

5. Mason to [Mr. ----- Brent?], 2 Oct. 1778, ibid, 1:436.

6. Mason to Washington, 14 Oct. 1775, ibid., 1:255.

7. Ibid., 1:278.

8. R. A. Rutland, *George Mason: Reluctant Statesman* (Baton Rouge: Louisiana State University Press, 1961; 1980 reprint), 54.

9. Rutland, *Papers of Mason*, 1:159; "To the Honorable the General Assembly of the Commonwealth of Virginia / A Memorial and Remonstrance," [ca. 20 June 1785], William T. Hutchinson et al., eds., *The Papers of James Madison*, 14 vols. to date (Chicago: University of Chicago Press and Charlottesville: The University Press of Virginia, 1962—), 8:304.

10. [Thomas Gordon and John Trenchard], *Cato's Letters*, 2 vols. (London: n.p., 1724), 1:97.

11. Leland's objections to the Constitution were copied and sent to Madison (Hutchinson, *Papers of Madison*, 10:541n. 2); *Documentary History of the Constitution of the United States*, 5 vols. (Washington: U.S. Department of State Library: 1894–1895), 4:526–28. Spelling has been modernized.

12. See James Morton Smith, *Freedom's Fetters* (Ithaca: Cornell University Press, 1956), 277–417.

13. Leonard Levy, *Jefferson & Civil Liberties: The Darker Sider* (Cambridge: Harvard University Press, 1963), 59.

14. Hutchinson, *Papers of Madison*, 12:207.

15. Ibid.

16. 3 Howard 609.

17. 283 U.S. 697.

18. Rutland, *Papers of Mason*, 3:1172.

19. *Near* v. *Minnesota*, 283 U.S. 697. For an excellent recent survey of the subject, see Henry J. Abraham, *Freedom and the Court: Civil Rights and Liberties in the United States*, fourth ed. (New York: Oxford University Press, 1982).

20. Quoted in Catherine L. Albanese, *Sons of the Fathers: The Civil Religion of the American Revolution* (Philadelphia: Temple University Press, 1976), viii.

21. Charles Pinckney to Madison, 14 Sept. 1801 (National Archives, Record Group 59: Diplomatic Despatches, Spain, vol. 6).

2

Religious Freedom: As Amended by the Founding Mothers

ROSEMARY KELLER
Associate Professor of Religion and American Culture
Garrett-Evangelical Theological Seminary

THE AMERICAN REVOLUTION OF THE LATE EIGHTEENTH CENTURY brought with it a new vision of "space" that would powerfully form the American experience. Obviously, the most explicit meaning of space related to the severed tie between Great Britain and the American colonies. Now an independent United States would be formed. Further, much of the story of American nationhood, even until the mid-20th century, has been the drama of geographical space—moving westward, conquering the continental boundaries, and then extending those borders thousands of miles beyond the mainland.

But the Founding Fathers envisioned another kind of space—the inward, personal expansion of human rights, which was embodied in the Virginia Declaration of Rights, the Declaration of Independence, and the Constitution of the United States. Both the vision and the trauma of the struggle for human rights, which have so deeply formed our American character, are embodied in the person of George Mason.

As his home, Gunston Hall, demonstrates, Mason bore the distinguishing characteristics of the Virginia aristocracy, including Washington, Jefferson, and Madison, who wrote the founding documents of Virginia and the American nation. Born in 1725, seven years before Washington and eighteen years before Jefferson, Mason was a member of the group of large landholders that held unquestioned social and political power in Virginia. Educated for the most part at home, Mason was steeped in the Enlightenment foundations of the nature of humanity and the purpose of government. He read widely in the standard texts of law and of ancient and English history, epecially regarding the concepts of natural rights.

His education, along with the social position, wealth, and political legacy of his family, led Mason to become an active participant in the Revolutionary cause from its inception. As a member of the convention to write the first constitution of the State of Virginia, Mason led a committee in preparing the Declaration of Rights to precede the Virginia Constitution. The Declaration of Rights, written in 1776, embodied the vision and stern warning that the rights of people came before the rights of government. The fundamental protections of the individual in the Declaration of Rights included the guarantees of trial by jury, free exercise of religion, free press, prohibition against standing armies, civilian control of the military, bail, and cruel and unusual punishments—all of which became the fundamental rights of the Declaration of Independence and the American Constitution. Mason also played an important part at the Constitutional Convention in 1787, and refused to sign the final version because, among other matters, it contained no bill of rights. His tenacious opposition to constitutional ratification by Virginia on those grounds led to ratification—based on the promise that the new government would add a bill of rights, as Congress did in its first session.

Yet the vision of human rights held by the Founding Fathers was much more expansive than the dimensions of human freedom that would be realized in their own day—or that they would even seek to fulfill in their generation. When George Mason developed the clause proclaiming the equality of all persons, many gentlemen freeholders opposed it, fearing it would incite slaves to rebellion. Mason himself knew that slaves did not have rights equivalent to those held by white persons, that free blacks were not equal to whites before the law, and that slavery was wrong. For Mason, as for other plantation owners and statesmen, his knowledge of "the good, the just, and the right," conflicted with economic gain.[1]

The founding documents of the United States, however, laid the foundation upon which human rights could be realized—and continue to be realized—into our own day. Certainly, this is true of the principle of religious freedom, the focus of this essay.

The great traditions of the American churches that developed in the 19th and 20th centuries grew out of the religious heritage of the American Revolution. This heritage was grounded in the principle of *religious freedom* formulated by George Mason in the Declaration of Rights and the Bill of Rights, guaranteeing that persons may worship according to the dictates of their own conscience. Gains in that direction had been made prior to the War for Independence. By 1775, toleration verging on freedom had become a fundamental part of the long-term American Revolution being enacted in the colonies. Guarantees of religious liberty first established in the Virginia Declaration of Rights set the pace and accelerated progress during the Revolutionary era. The disestablishment of American churches, *separation of church and state,* was a close correlate of religious freedom. The most decisive act for disestablishment during the Revolutionary era was passed in Virginia, though the state-church relationships were severed by the end of the era in all states except Massachusetts, Connecticut, and New Hampshire—the last coming in Massachusetts in 1833.

Denominationalism followed naturally upon principles of religious freedom and separation of church and state. Negatively stated, it repudiated the idea that Christians under any government must be comprehended into a "true" church. Positively, denominationalism affirmed that the diversity of communions and theological perspectives enriched the church as the whole body of Jesus Christ. Religious freedom led also to *voluntaryism,* the committed voluntary support of laypersons for church government, programming, and mission work. Voluntaryism brought with it more democratically-based principles of local church organization, tendencies to downplay vested authority in hierarchical systems of church government, and the decline of power and status centered in the minister. Responsibilities and authority were to be shared more evenly by both clergy and laity. Finally, a national spirit combining patriotic and religious feeling, known as *civil religion,* came into existence. In its highest form, civil religion posited that the nation, with its liberties and guaranteed rights of humankind, including religious freedom, had a special destiny given it by God.[2]

These have been the traditional meanings and long-term implications of religious freedom in America. This essay, however, will explore a part of the "underside" of the story of religious freedom: the heritage of the "founding mothers" from the Colonial and Revolutionary periods. This story is only beginning to be recovered, and my perspective grows primarily out of research recently brought together in the second volume of *Women and Religion in America,* which has been edited by Rosemary Ruether and myself and to which eight other scholars have contributed primary source documents and analytical essays.[3] The term "founding mothers" will refer here to the broad spectrum of women in Colonial and Revolutionary America, from New England to the southern colonies, and to the lives of black and native American women, and females of French and Spanish extraction, as well as to white women of English background. This essay will focus on the basic issues that emerge through the diverse experience of women in a variety of cultures in Colonial and Revolutionary America. Their lives demonstrate the inadequacy of traditional meanings and effects of religious freedom when applied to the experience of women.

Most native American women who were reached by European missionaries grafted selective aspects of Christianity onto their own religious traditions, a process that continues even today, and remained in the Indian villages of their origin for their entire lives. Indian women and men exhibited far more willingness to penetrate the mysteries of European Christianity than was true in reverse. A number of 17th and 18th century American Indian women turned to Christianity with a fervor and intellectual intensity so convincing as to astound European-American missionaries and lay observers. They shared in common an active quest for Christian understanding and grace, whether through a rigorous education under a priest, minister or nun; self-mortification, fasting, and prayer culminating in a conversion experience akin, perhaps, to an Indian vision quest; vows of chastity; good works, a persistent attempt to convert family and friends; or a combination of all these.[4]

Conversion to Christianity meant spiritual liberation for some Indian women. The experience of Jerusha Ompan, an Algonquian speaking woman who lived on Martha's Vineyard and was raised as a Christian, testifies to her new inner life. Further, a sense of ministry by Jerusha to her family and friends emerges from the pages of a biographical sketch of her written before her death at twenty-nine in 1711. The account by Experience Mayhew, Puritan missionary in her village, indicates the depth of Jerusha's theological insight and the instruction that she gave to others:

> She used to ask serious Questions in Matters of Religion, as particularly of one she enquired, Whether *Adam* had Freewill before his Fall, and how his Sin came to be imputed and propagated to his Posterity, and how we might be delivered from it? And, lastly, how she ought to order her Prayers with respect to it? . . .
>
> Some of her Relations that survive her, do testify concerning her, that she was a serious and faithful Reprover of their sinful Miscarriages, and that she did often give them good Counsel; particularly one of her Brothers, that was younger than she, gives this Testimony concerning her; and says also that she used to instruct him in his Catechism.
>
> She was about 29 Years old before she dy'd; and tho she had some Offers of Marriage made to her, yet she would accept of none of them, alledging to her Friends as the reason of her Refusal, that of the Aposles [*sic*] in the first Epistle to the *Corrinthians* [*sic*], *Chap. vii. The unmarried Woman careth for the Things of the Lord, &c.*
>
> Her Discourses were during that time very pious edifying; particularly she declared, that she saw no Beauty in the most desirable things and Enjoyment of this World, and wished that all her Relations and Friends had the same Sentiments concerning them as she had. She talked of Heaven as a Place of transcendent Excellency and Glory, and manifested earnest Desires of going to that Place. She declared that if she were clothed with the Righteousness of Christ, that would entitle her to the Blessedness which was to be enjoyed in the Kingdom of God; and that *his Ressurrection* [*sic*] would preserve her from a State of Sin and Death, to an eternal Life of Glory. She exhorted her Relations and Visitors to be diligent Seekers of God, and to depart from all Iniquity.[5]

Yet the effects of Christianization on American Indian women were complex. When travelers, settlers, and missionaries came to North America in the early Colonial period, they confronted indigenous Indian cultures in which Indian women played diverse roles in tribal religious life. Each of the competing Christian churches vied for the souls of American Indians and imposed upon them their various religious cultures. Thus, Indians were not just Christianized; they were turned into Counter-Reformation French Catholics in Quebec, Counter-Reformation Spanish Catholics in Mexico, German-speaking Moravian Brethren in Pennsylvania, and English Puritans in New England. Each European nation and sect in part justified its divine mission through its claims to evangelize the Indians. Thus, Indian women went through an astonishing plurality of metamorphoses throughout the colonies as each church group claimed success in evangelization by making Indians over into their own culture image. American Indian women had prominent roles in the traditions, ceremonies, and rituals of indigenous tribal life. It would appear that they often enjoyed greater opportunity for independent religious thought and ceremonial participation than did their American and European counterparts until at least the mid-nineteenth century. Nevertheless, conversion to Christianity may, in some cases, have meant constriction of religious freedom for Indian women.[6]

It is notable, however, that Indians became capable of confronting whites with their failure to practice their own religious precepts. The story of Indian women who requested to speak at the Council of the Six Nations with the American government in western New York in 1794 is revealing. In response to an earlier visit by the woman preacher, Jemima Wilkinson, to the Council, in which she had called upon the Indians to repent of their sins, the Indian women called upon the whites to repent of their grievous sins of oppressing the

Indians and taking their lands. William Savery, a Quaker missionary, described the directness and boldness of the Indian women's words as he heard them at the Council meeting:

> Being about to proceed to business, a request was made from three Indian women to be admitted to the council and deliver their sentiments, which being granted, they were introduced by Red Jacket. He addressed himself to the sachems and warriors, desiring their indulgence of the women, and also to the commissioner, enforcing their request by observing, that the other day one of our women had liberty to speak in council. He was then desired to act as orator for the women, and deliver to the council what they had to say. The substance of this was, that they felt a deep interest in the affairs of their nation, and having heard the opinions of their sachems, they fully concurred in them, that the white people had been the cause of all the Indians' distresses; that they had pressed and squeezed them together, until it had [caused] them great pain at their hearts, and that the whites ought to give them back the lands they had taken from them. That one of the white women had yesterday told the Indians to repent; and they now called on the white people to repent, for they had as much need as the Indians, and that they should wrong the Indians no more.[7]

The convent life, brought to North America by both the French and Spanish nuns of the Roman Catholic Church, offered native American converts a sphere of assured social respect, comfort, some autonomy and education—a larger scope for the talents of an independent woman who wished to pursue intellectual advancement, adventure, and high commitment to Christian ideals. The brilliant Renaissance humanist, scholar, and poet, Sor Juana Inez de la Cruz, was an example of an upper-class Spanish woman of the literate class in New Spain who chose a religious life over marriage. Of the two options open to "respectable" women in her culture, the convent life offered her a larger sphere for educational development than did marriage. Sor Juana lived most of her life as a professed nun in the Hieronimite Convent of San Geronimo in Mexico City and reached her prime as a writer within the orthodox confines of the institutional religious order. She encountered much opposition to her activities, however, from within the church itself. In one of her famous works, "Response to Sor Filotea de la Cruz," pen name of the Bishop of Puebla, she defended both her own literary vocation and the right of all women to use their intellect, since nothing in the Catholic Church expressly forbade them to do so. Her statement, written to church authorities in the late 17th century, identifies her as one of the earliest advocates of women's right to their full and true personhood.[8]

Though Sor Juana may have been a lonely voice in the Roman Catholic Church, the struggle for religious freedom was at the heart of the relationship between church renewal and the place of women in early Puritan society of 17th century New England. Men and women of first generation New England Puritanism were the product of a dissenting culture that was at war with the established Anglican Church. The splintering of the English Reformation into an array of competing sects reflected the conflicts of social classes as well as religious viewpoints. In this atmosphere of incipient civil war, women often took the initiative in gathering dissenting congregations, calling ministers, and asserting their own rights to preach and to administer churches. Dissenting ministers encouraged such independence in women when the foe was the established church.

However, once the dissenting clergy became ministers of the established Puritan Church of New England, their interpretation of religious liberty changed sharply. While still at sea before landing in Massachusetts Bay, John Winthrop described his vision of the religious community that the Puritans were about to establish as a world without conflict, dissension, and strife, an organic society in which all would "be knitt together in this worke as one man." They were to "enjoy the liberties of the gospel in purity with peace." The word liberty did not imply freedom of conscience in religious belief, however, but freedom to obey the will of God and to restore God's order in a chaotic world. Such a vision depended upon a highly structured hierarchical society in which all people knew their places and voluntarily chose to stay in them.[9]

Puritan theory assigned a positive but limited place to women as helpmeets to their husbands and co-authorities over children and servants, under their husbands. It encouraged the active piety of lay women as docile recipients of Puritan preaching and piety. Accommodation of women to their socially prescribed subordination was essential to the maintenance of the Puritan order, and most women probably assumed that position without question. No space was available for the woman whose religious experiences bypassed ministerial authority and who sought to define her own faith.[10]

Strains in the social order occurred even within the first generation of Puritan settlement because a considerable number of women applied the implications of radical spiritual equality and freedom in St. Paul to themselves. Their primary text, one that had empowered the radical sectarians of the English Reformation, was Galatians 3:28: "There is neither Jew nor Greek, bond nor free, male nor female: for you are all one in Christ Jesus."

Until recently, the "Anne Hutchinson Affair" has been held up as an anomaly, an example of a single insubordinate and rebellious woman who stood out strikingly against a background of general conformity by New England women. Hutchinson contended both that grace came to individuals directly from God and that New England clergy were not fit ministers of the gospel. She then proceeded to hold private meetings in her home, where she taught her beliefs to men and women of the Boston church. Her views and actions were a direct challenge to the theological base and political power structure of the Puritan order—and to the Puritan meaning of religious freedom. Anne Hutchinson's bold and radical application, that spiritual equality and freedom before God sanctioned social equality and freedom of women alongside men on earth, brought a judgment from her inquisitors that her behavior was neither "tolerable nor comely in the sight of God nor fitting for your sex," and resulted in her banishment from the colony.[11]

Deeper investigation indicates that Anne Hutchinson was simply the symbol, and probably the impetus, for a larger number of women and of female circles in Boston, Salem, New Haven, and possibly other New England towns, who challenged religious and sexual subordination. Their activism was a direct affront to the view of religious freedom held by John Winthrop, which meant that all persons were to obey God's will and bring about God's plan in the same way. Throughout the 17th century, women who dissented from the authority of minister, magistrate or husband were branded heretics and often deemed witches as well. They were condemned as heretics because woman's place in society was divinely ordained and revealed in Scripture. To revolt against the established order was to rebel against God and God's revealed Will. They were branded as witches because only the promptings of the Devil could explain such insubordination in a woman.[12]

Trials against women for heresy and witchcraft swept across the New England colonies from the mid-17th century until the end of the century. The two kinds of trials were not isolated cases. The charges were generally interconnected, and often the women charged were members of female circles in which they established close relationships. They must be interpreted against the background of a dramatic struggle between the spirit of autonomy released by the dissenting wing of the English Reformation and a male leadership that had no place in its theology or society for women who applied this autonomy to themselves.[13]

By the end of the 17th century the heresy and witchcraft trials had abated, perhaps less because their presuppositions were discredited than because the ministry had won its struggle to repress women and to place them within its own definition of their place in society and the church. Here we find the Puritan preacher encouraging the active lay piety of women in the congregation, so long as women took their cues from the preacher and confined their evangelizing zeal to the private sphere of family and home.[14]

The settled domestic piety of women primarily characterized the world and the vision of southern white women's religious life in the Colonial period. Most of these women belonged to the established Anglican Church, although there were also Catholic women in Maryland, Jewish women in New York and the Carolinas and an increasing number of women entering dissenting churches. They were encouraged to practice a devout but moderate piety within the limits of their homes as mentors of their children and servants. They were also instructed to evangelize their husbands discreetly. Wive were, of course, not to take authority over husbands but to endure patiently, even though their husbands might be impious, unfaithful, or even abusive.

By the 18th century, women were clearly thought to have a more religious nature than men. This aspect of their personalities, tied to their long ingrained low self-esteem underscored by the legacy of Eve and their domestic world, closely defined the boundaries of women's lives. Though religion did not offer most women an alternative to their inherited life cycle, it did prove to be the one means of providing them some "space" to gain a more secure identity by cultivating their individuality. It encouraged women to have private devotions, to write out religious exercises, and to develop their own prayers. A diary could become an expression of religious sentiment and an awakening of the self.[15]

Although teaching their children catechism and prayers was a primary function, a part of the religious experience of many southern women was the instruction of their slaves in Christian principles. If many white women were illiterate, black women had a much more difficult time obtaining any reading and writing skills unless they had mistresses who allowed it to happen—and often in a secretive atmosphere.[16]

Many women, whites as well as blacks, experienced the contagious effect of the message of spiritual equality preached by ministers of the Great Awakening. By 1800, a number of women, sometimes over husbands' objections, were participating in revivals and joining the Baptists and Methodists. Historians have recently pointed out the number of women who joined evangelical denominations in the early nineteenth century. This move, however, was already beginning in the South in the Revolutionary era. In revivals and evangelical church services, women no longer played a secondary role but were on an equal footing with men. One Regular Baptist preacher objected to the ordination of Daniel Marshall on these grounds: "that he believed them [Separate Baptists] to be a disorderly sect suffering women to pray in public, and permitting every ignorant man to preach that chose: that they encouraged noise and confusion in their meetings." Marshall's wife, the sister of revivalist Shubal Stearns, also preached, which must have both amazed and irritated the Regular Baptists even more. Semple thought her, however, a "lady of good sense, singular piety, and surprising elocution." On countless occasions, she had "melted a whole concourse into tears, by prayers and exhortations."[17]

The evangelical denominations could provide women with an emotional outlet and identity that other groups could not. They could also bring black and white women together. A Presbyterian minister described one revival in North Carolina where he walked near "a black-woman grasping her mistress' hand and crying 'O Mistress you prayed for me when I wanted a heart to pray for myself. Now thank God he has given me a heart to pray for you and everybody else'."[18]

Religion provided southern white women meaning and order in their lives. Although it did not provide public identity and roles for many women, it did begin to give them a degree of spiritual liberation that was increased by their participation in evangelical denominations. The ambiguity of the relationship between white Christian wives and black slaves was a reality of their religious experience. In theory, white women should see their servants as a part of their households and extend their evangelizing nurture to them, so that mistress, children, and servants would kneel together in prayer at the close of the day. In fact, many slaves preferred to become Baptists or Methodists, attracted both to the more lively styles of worship and to the greater communal autonomy found in the dissenting churches. White women were caught between the male religious and social authorities and the enslaved black world. They were themselves subjects and victims of its hierarchical social order; they were also agents of it who struggled, not always successfully, to enculturate their slaves in its values.

Black women, brought as slaves to North America in the seventeenth and eighteenth centuries, had been persons in their own right, with responsibilities and privileges not always based on husbands' and fathers' patriarchal powers in their West African tribes. They had controlled marketplaces and their economic monopoly provided them with leverage for autonomous activity and opportunities for leadership experiences. In religious ceremonies, for instance, women frequently were priests and leaders of cults.[19]

African women's initial experience with the churches in North America was one of exclusion from church membership. The increasing tendency of colonial Christianity to idealize white women as the "religious and moral sex" seldom was extended to black women. They were regarded as naturally immoral, "beastly," and little fitted to Christian religiosity.

The Anglican-dominated legislature in Virginia enacted a law that distinguished between servants. European servants were designated "Christian," and American laborers were referred to as "Negro [implying non-Christian] servants." Colonial plantation owners underscored the distinction by neglecting to bring "Negro servants" into the Christian church, sometimes legislating against black church attendance, and resisting the demands of churches and missionary societies to evangelize Africans because they feared that baptism would give the slave rights to emancipation.

For at least one black woman, Elizabeth Key, baptism had brought her freedom. She was the daughter of an Englishman, Thomas Key, and an unknown slave woman in early Virginia. In 1656, she brought suit in the Northumberland County Court for her freedom on the basis that her father was a free man, that she had been baptized a Christian, and that she had been sold for a definite period of time. If the case had occurred six years later, there would have been no question about her status; she would have taken the condition of her mother. In this case, Elizabeth's Christian faith helped to determine her freedom.[20]

By the early 1660s, however, Massachusetts, Virginia, and other English colonies had taken steps to make slavery a legally self-perpetuating institution. Intending to settle the question of whether converted slaves should or could be freed, Virginia passed legislation in 1662 stating that children would inherit their mothers' social status—not their religious condition. Still not certain whether Christians could be enslaved, however, in the absence of an English law positively stating that, Virginia enacted legislation prohibiting a slave's status from being altered because he or she was baptized. It remained for some Christian theologians to argue that the Scriptures allowed slavery, and so it was compatible with Christianity to baptize persons and yet hold as slaves those who were regarded as lacking full human status.[21]

Only in 1701 did the leadership within the Church of England organize a united drive to evangelize and teach among slaves. A missionary band, the Society for the Propagation of the Gospel in Foreign Parts, was formed, which operated out of London and was financially independent of local church parishes. Although the Society owned slaves in its early years and took the position that emancipation was not a mandatory result of conversion, settlers were suspicious that the intentions of the Society were to initiate the first step toward freedom for black slaves.[22]

The Great Awakenings, which highlighted American sectarianism and fragmented activity of the Anglican Society for the Propagation of the Gospel in Foreign Parts around the mid-eighteenth century, also provided African/Afro-Americans with their first virtually unrestricted participation in Christianity in North America. During the religious ferment and widespread conversion experiences, white anti-slavery sentiment and black assertiveness intensified. In 1743, for example, a black woman and her husband sued a white man for trespassing upon her character. They made clear their understanding that a Christian woman's (including a black woman's) moral reputation should not be impugned without legal challenge.[23]

Popular evangelists of the Great Awakening, such as

George Whitefield, commented on the enthusiasm with which Negroes, particularly women, received the Gospel and its messengers. John Wesley, himself an antislavery advocate, noted in his *Diary* that the first Methodist in New York City was a "Negro Servant" named Betty. Sentiment against slave conversions still abounded, and circuit riders had to urge owners to send slaves to religious instruction and to worship. Quakers and other antislavery groups increased their proclamations and other active challenges to the institution of slavery.

African women adopted Christianity with alacrity. With the disintegration of African communal identity, the adoption of Christianity offered the only hope for black mothers to find a new identity for themselves and their children. During the First Great Awakening, blacks flocked particularly to the Methodists and Baptists, attracted, among other things, to the antislavery message that was at least hinted in these circles, although even the Quakers were seldom forthright in their opposition to slavery as an institution. Even these dissenting churches, however, seldom extended full and equal fellowship to their black converts, and so, by the end of the Colonial period, American black Christians began to break with these churches and to found black congregations and denominations. Although preaching authority was not officially extended to women even in black churches, black women began to find ministerial roles as missionaries, charitable workers, and educators within these black denominations.[24]

In the diverse religious scene of Colonial America, the heirs of the Radical Reformation also were to be found. From the English in the seventeenth century there flowed Quaker missionaries, exponents of radical spiritualist Puritanism. From Germany came a diversity of Pietist sects, often adopting communal social forms and some of them practicing celibacy. These groups were more experimental in their theology and social practices toward women. The Quakers, through their co-founder, Margaret Fell, and her daughters, developed a theology and exegesis of women's spiritual equality. They advocated women's right both to preach and evangelize and to participate in church administration. The Quakers preserved and developed the emancipatory trends of dissenting Puritanism. Not surprisingly, they were drawn into confrontation with the Puritan authorities in Massachusetts who were engaged in repressing these emancipatory trends in their own Christian social order. Several were finally hanged. The sufferings of Quaker women in this struggle with Puritan theocracy form a heroic chapter of early Quakerism in America.

A controversial innovation in early Quakerism was the institution of Women's Meetings, which gave Quaker women an official role in the administration and government of the Society. Women's Meetings both supervised internal morality and managed extensive works of charity. They gathered and administered funds for the relief of the imprisoned, the poor, the sick, widows, orphans, and the aged. They organized projects, such as spinning groups, for unemployed women and placed orphans in apprenticeships. They supervised marriages and tithe paying within the society.[25]

The 18th century saw a downplaying of the role of Women's Meetings and women as ministers. But the advocacy of women's spiritual and administrative powers remained strong enough in the nineteenth century to attract an early feminist, Sarah Grimké, into the Quaker fold in Philadelphia in 1821. It is not accidental that a number of the early feminists and abolitionists of the nineteenth century, such as Lucretia Mott and Susan B. Anthony, were Quaker ministers.[26]

Among the German Pietist sects, the Ephrata community of Pennsylvania and the Moravian Brethren form two notable types. In both, women had a fixed and settled place. The forthright confrontation with religious authority found in the Puritan and Quaker context finds no echo among these German groups. Yet the German sects also created a large sphere for woman's religious and administrative abilities through their communal social order. We also find in these sects experimentation with the doctrines of God and anthropology that has its roots in the Christian mystical and gnostic traditions. God is believed to have a feminine as well as a masculine side, and celibacy is seen as restoring androgynous wholeness to fallen humanity.[27]

A similar theology is found among the Anglo-American Shakers, who were led to the American shores by Mother Ann Lee in 1786. For the Shakers also, God is androgynous. They take this idea a step farther by arguing that there must be a female as well as male Messiah to represent redeemed humanity and the dual aspects of God. The American Revolution offered a scene of social conflict in which radically new religious voices were heard. Among them was the New England preacher, Jemima Wilkinson, who, after her "resurrection" experience, styled herself the "Universal Public Friend" and claimed messianic authority to preach God's final word of redemption in the "last days."

These Anglo-American women of radical sectarian groups reveal emancipatory hopes and visions released by the English Reformation and renewed again during the American Revolution. In contrast to established patriarchal theory, which continued to be espoused by established forms of Protestantism, these groups suggest that women might claim equal spiritual authority and even become the chosen instruments of God to preach salvation and found churches of the new millenial order.[28]

The evangelical revival that swept the American churches in the 18th century from New England to the Southern colonies renewed some of the emancipatory potential of radical

Christianity that was found earlier among the antinomian Puritans and the Quakers. Revivalism also bypassed established ecclesiastical authority by stressing direct personal experience of God's redeeming grace. In this drama of repentance and conversion, social distinctions melted away. Women, unequal in society, were spiritually equal before God as repentant sinners and a divine grace.[29]

Thus in the evangelical and revival movements in America, even prior to the American Revolution, the trend was accentuated that had begun in late 17th and early 18th century Puritan preaching. This growing stress on woman's moral superiority, her greater religiosity, and her role as domestic evangelist, created mixed messages for women in the evangelical movements. Woman was, at once, man's spiritual equal, and, in some way, his superior and yet his social subordinate. This created conflicting directions for woman's role in the church. On the one hand, woman's piety was still seen as directing her to voluntary acceptance of her subordination in church and society. On the other hand, the stress on her religiousness and evangelizing mission tended to break these limits and direct woman's ministry into a widening sphere that led her from the family circle into prayer circles of friends and finally to becoming organizers and even preachers at revival meetings. Early Methodism particularly demonstrated these mixed messages of the evangelical movement for women and gave us intimations of those evangelical women of the Wesleyan tradition who, in the nineteenth century, would increasingly claim the right to preach.

Finally, what was the relationship among women, religious freedom, and the American Revolutionary War? The revolutionary commitment of the founding fathers and mothers of patriot persuasion was grounded in an image of the American nation as a divinely appointed instrument of political emancipation. Both the rationalist traditions of the Enlightenment and the results of the evangelical revivalist fervor transformed the meaning of the war into a religious commitment, a Battle of the Lord in which God ordained an American victory. As "Daughters of Liberty" who supported the American Revolutionary army through their sewing bees and fundraising, women were enthusiastic advocates of the revolutionary struggle.[30]

Yet, again, as in the Reformation, the ideology of equality, shaped by men in their conflicts with established authority, was not intended to be extended to women and other dependent persons. White propertied males were the subjects of that "equality of human nature," from which, according to the Declaration of Independence, there flow equal civil rights. The pleas of Abigail Adams to her husband, John, at the Continental Congress, to "Remember the Ladies" went unheeded. John Adams's letters, however, indicate that he, like George Mason and other founding fathers, realized the far-reaching ramifications of religious freedom and human rights which they had implied in the Declaration of Independence, the Virginia Declaration of Rights, and the United States Constitution. Perhaps they knew that these rights must one day be extended to minority groups and individuals.[31]

The most immediate implication of women's religious experience during the American Revolution and early 19th century was development of the role of republican womanhood and motherhood. Such an understanding elevated public virtue—disinterested secular service growing out of honesty, integrity, and moral values—to a religious principle. Women, as guardians of the home, became the primary bearers, responsible for inculcating virtue into their sons, daughters, and even husbands. Such a purpose for women justified a broader education for them but one that would focus their purpose within the home, not in professional service in society.[32]

Thus, the period between the Reformation and the American Revolution presented conflicting realities of religious freedom for women in Colonial and Revolutionary America. Women enthusiastically responded to and participated in renewal movements, helped evangelize Indians and settle a new continent. But the emancipatory messages of these movements were contradicted by growing restrictions on the actual social mobility and economic roles of women from a sixteenth-century feudal, peasant, and merchant society into an industrialized nineteenth-century world. Women's roles in the home would become more restricted as their lives became directed into narrower and more intensive roles as wives and mothers in the home. Religious institutions and ideologies would, simultaneously, exalt woman's piety and seek to restrict it to this shrinking world.

Yet the evangelical mandate to women to bring souls to Christ and the liberal ideology of religious freedom and human rights have long range liberating effects. Again and again, in the 19th and 20th centuries, they would provide the foundation for religious movements and religious sanctions in society for the attainment of God-given inalienable rights and functions of women alongside men in both the sacred and secular spheres and the private and public realms of life.

Notes

1. For information regarding George Mason, my thanks to Josephine F. Pacheco, *George Mason: the Man, the University* (Fairfax, Virginia: George Mason University, n.d.).

2. Sydney E. Ahlstrom, *A Religious History of the American People,* 2 vols. (Garden City, New York: Doubleday and Co., 1975), 1:459–465.

3. Rosemary R. Ruether and Rosemary S. Keller, eds., *Women and Religion in America,* 2 vols. (San Francisco: Harper & Row,

1981, 1983) vol. 2. The basic theses of this essay grow out of the perspectives developed more fully in this volume by the several contributors to whom I am indebted: Jacqueline Peterson, Mary Druke, Asunción Lavrin, Christine Allen, Alice Mathews, Lillian Webb, Catherine Prelinger, and Martha Blauvelt, as well as Rosemary Ruether and myself.

4. James P. Ronda and James Axtell, *Indian Missions: A Critical Bibliography*, The Newberry Library Center for the History of the American Indian Bibliographical Series (Bloomington: University of Indiana Press, 1978) is a helpful introduction to the literature on missionary activity among North American Indians. Also see Henry Warner Bowden, *American Indians and Christian Missions: Studies in Cultural Conflict* (Chicago: University of Chicago Press, 1981).

5. *Indian Converts: or, Some Account of the Lives and Dying Speeches of a Considerable Number of the Christianized Indians of Martha's Vineyard, in New England, by Experience Mayhew* (London: Printed for Samuel Gerrish, Bookseller in Boston in New England, and sold by J. Osborn and T. Longman in Pater-noster-Row, 1727), 175–179.

6. The analysis of Jacqueline Peterson and Mary Druke in Chapter 1, "American Indian Women and Religion," in Ruether and Keller, *Women and Religion in America*, vol. 2, leads to this conclusion.

7. *A Journal of the Life, Travels and Religious Labors of William Savery* (London: C. Gilpin, 1844), 66, 68–70.

8. Juana Inéz de la Cruz, "Respuesta a Sor Juana Inéz de la Cruz," in *A Woman of Genius: The Intellectual Autobiography of Sor Juana Inéz de la Cruz*, trans. and intro. by Margaret Sayers Peden (Salisbury, Connecticut: Lime Rock Press, Inc., 1982). Excerpts from the *Autobiography* are found in document #8, Asunción Lavrin, "Women and Religion in Spanish America," Ruether and Keller, *Women and Religion in America*, 2:65–68.

9. John Winthrop, "A Modell of Christian Charity," in Perry Miller and Thomas H. Johnson, eds., 2 vols. *The Puritans: A Sourcebook of Their Writings* (New York: Harper & Row, 1963) 1:195–199; David D. Hall, *The Faithful Shepherd* (Chapel Hill: The University of North Carolina Press, 1972), Chapters 4, 5.

10. Carol F. Karlsen, "The Devil in the Shape of a Woman: The Witch in Seventeenth Century New England," unpublished PhD

dissertation, Yale University, 1980; Gerald F. Moran, "'Sisters' in Christ: Women and the Church in Seventeenth Century New England," in Janet W. James, ed., *Women in American Religion* (Philadelphia: University of Pennsylvania Press, 1980), 47–65.

11. David D. Hall, *The Antinomian Controversy, 1636–1638: A Documentary History* (Middletown, Connecticut: Wesleyan University Press, 1968); Lyle Koehler, "The Case of the American Jezebels: Anne Hutchinson and Female Agitation during the Years of Antinomian Turmoil, 1636–1640," *William and Mary Quarterly*, 3rd Series, 31 (Jan. 1974), 55–78; Koehler, *A Search for Power* (Urbana: University of Illinois Press, 1980); Ben Barker-Benfield, "Anne Hutchinson and the Puritan Attitude Toward Women," *Feminist Studies*, 1, (Fall, 1972) unnumbered.

12. Examples and documentation of the wider circles of female dissenters are drawn together by Rosemary Keller, "New England Women: Ideology and Experience in First-Generation Puritanism (1630–1650)," Chapter 4 in Ruether and Keller, *Women and Religion in America*, vol. 2.

13. Karlsen, "The Devil in the Shape of a Woman."

14. John Cotton, "Singing of Psalms a Gospel Ordinance, 1650," in Edmund Clarence Stedman and Ellen Mackey Hutchinson, eds., *A Library of American Literature from the Earliest Settlement to the Present Time* (New York: Charles L. Webster & Co., 1888), 1:254–270.

15. This reality is documented in the experience of Southern women through their own writings, such as Elise Pinckney and Marvin R. Zahniser, eds., *The Letterbook of Eliza Lucas Pinckney, 1739–1762* (Chapel Hill: The University of North Carolina Press, 1972); The Journal of Betsy Foote Washington, Oct. 1789, Washington Family Papers, Library of Congress, Manuscripts Division, Washington, D.C.; Papers of Margaret Sharpe Gaston in the William Gaston Papers in the Southern Historical Collection of the University of North Carolina Library, Chapel Hill; David Ramsay, ed., *Memoirs of the Life of Martha Laurens Ramsay . . .* (Charlestown: Samuel Etheridge, 1812); also see Alice Mathews, "The Religious Experience of Southern Women in the Colonial and Revolutionary Eras," Chapter 5, in Ruether and Keller, *Women and Religion in America*, vol. 2, and Donald Mathews, *Religion in the Old South* (Chicago: University of Chicago Press, 1977).

16. American Correspondence, Dr. Bray's Associates, Feb. 16, 1761, 120–121; Extracts of letters from Minute Book of Dr. Bray's Associates, I: 180, Oct. 7, 1766; 186, March 3, 1763; 243, April 3, 1766; II: 71, 72, March 2, 1775, photocopies in the Library of Congress Manuscripts Division, Washington, D.C.

17. Robert B. Semple, *A History of the Rise and Progress of the Baptists in Virginia* (Richmond, Virginia: John O'Lynch, 1810), 5, 374.

18. James Hall, *A Narrative of a Most Extraordinary Work of Religion in North Carolina* (Philadelphia: William W. Woodward, 1802), 20–22, 24.

19. John S. Mbiti, *African Religions and Philosophies* (Garden City, New York: Doubleday & Co., 1970); Cheikh Anta Diop, *African Origin of Civilization,* Mercer Cook, trans. (New York: Laurence Hill & Co., 1974).

20. See Lillian Webb, "Black Women and Religion in the Colonial Period," Chapter 6, Ruether and Keller, *Women and Religion in America,* vol. 2.

21. William W. Hening, *Statutes at Large: Laws of Virginia* (New York: 1823), 2:260, for Act III.

22. Frank J. Klingberg, *Anglican Humanitarianism in Colonial New York* (Philadelphia: Church Historical Society, 1940).

23. Court record of case of *William and Elizabeth Hood versus Adam Jourdan,* Bucks County, Pennsylvania, Court of Quarter Session (September 1745), from Historical Society of Pennsylvania.

24. Absalom Jones and Richard Allen, "A Narrative of the Proceedings of the People During the Late Awful Calamity in Philadelphia, in the Year, 1793," in Dorothy Porter, ed., *Negro Protest Pamphlets* (New York: Arno, 1969), 9; Henry J. Cadbury, "Negro Membership in the Society of Friends," *Journal of Negro History* 21 (April 1936), 171.

25. See Rosemary R. Ruether, "Women in Sectarian and Utopian Groups," Chapter 7, Ruether and Keller, *Women and Religion in America,* vol. 2; Isabel Ross, *Margaret Fell: Mother of Quakerism* (London: Longmans, Green and Co., 1949), 283–302. Also see Mabel Brailsford, *Quaker Women, 1650–1690* (London: Duckworth and Co., 1915), 268–289.

26. Gerda Lerner, *The Grimké Sisters from South Carolina* (New York: Schocken, 1971), 57–59, 86; Otelia Cromwell, *Lucretia Mott*

(Cambridge, Massachusetts: Harvard University Press, 1958).

27. Eugene E. Doll, *The Ephrata Cloister: An Introduction* (Ephrata, Pennsylvania: Ephrata Cloister Associates, 1958–78), 22; Catherine F. Smith, "Jane Lead: The Feminist Mind and Art of a Seventeenth Century Protestant Mystic," in Rosemary R. Ruether and Eleanor McLoughlin, *Women of Spirit: Female Leadership in the Jewish and Christian Traditions* (New York: Simon and Schuster, 1979), 189; Walter C. Klein, *Johann Conrad Beissel: Mystic and Martinet 1690–1768* (Philadelphia: University of Pennsylvania Press, 1942), 195, 127.

28. Herbert Wisbey, Jr., *Pioneer Prophetess: Jemima Wilkinson, The Publick Universal Friend* (Ithaca: Cornell University Press, 1964) including bibliographical essay; Nardi R. Campion, *Ann the Word, Founder of the Shakers* (Boston: Little, Brown, 1976); *Testimonies of the Life, Character, Revelations and Doctrines of Mother Ann Lee and the Elders with Her, Through Whom the Word of Eternal Life Was Opened This Day of Christ's Second Appearing.* Collected from Living Witnesses in Union with the Church, ed. S. Y. Wells (Albany, New York: Packard and Benthuysen, 1827).

29. See Martha Blauvelt and Rosemary Keller, "Women and Revivalism: The Puritan and Wesleyan Traditions," Chapter 8 in Ruether and Keller, *Women and Religion in America,* vol. 2. Other useful secondary sources include James, ed., *Women in American Religion;* Lonna M. Malmsheimer, "Daughters of Zion: New England Roots of American Feminism," *New England Quarterly* 50 (1977), 484–505.

30. Mary Beth Norton, *Liberty's Daughters: The Revolutionary Experience of American Women, 1750–1800* (Boston: Little, Brown, 1980). Abigail Adams is a notable case study of the religious commitment which patriots vested in the American Revolution; see L. H. Butterfield, ed., *Adams Family Correspondence* (Cambridge, Massachusetts: Harvard University Press, 1963–), vols. 1–4; Rosemary Keller, *Abigail Adams and the American Revolution: A Personal History* (New York: Arno, 1981).

31. Keller, *Abigail Adams and the American Revolution,* Chapter 6; Bernard Bailyn, *The Ideological Origins of the American Revolution* (Cambridge, Massachusetts: Belknap Press, 1967); Gordon S. Wood, *The Creation of the American Republic, 1776–1787* (Chapel Hill: The University of North Carolina Press, 1969); Edmund S.

Morgan, *American Slavery, American Freedom* (New York: Norton and Co., 1975).

32. Linda Kerber, *Women of the Republic: Intellect and Ideology in Revolutionary America* (Chapel Hill: The University of North Carolina Press, 1980); Rosemary Keller, "Women, Civil Religion, and the American Revolution," Chapter 9 in Ruether and Keller, *Women and Religion in America*, vol. 2.

3

Free Speech and Its Philosophical Roots

FREDERICK SCHAUER
Cutler Professor of Law
College of William and Mary

I

WE ALL KNOW, OR AT LEAST WE SHOULD ALL KNOW, THAT GEORGE Mason, by being the principal author of the Virginia Declaration of Rights of 1776, was therefore the source and author of the world's first explicit legal protection of freedom of the press. The language is simple and bold: "That the freedom of the Press is one of the greatest bulwarks of liberty, and can never be restrained but by despotick Governments."[1] But Mason's reference to "*the* freedom of the Press," as well as the reference to "the freedom of speech, or of the press" in the First Amendment to the Constitution of the United States,[2] is neither crystal clear nor self-defining. Perhaps the most important word in both of these documents is "the," because the use of that word suggests that it is a particular condition that is in need of protection, rather than anything and everything that may happen to be produced by a printing press, in the case of the Virginia Declaration of Rights, or that may happen as well to be spoken, in the case of the First Amendment.[3] After all, it was possible, even in 1776, to produce a contract or deed by use of a printing press, and no one would now or then contend that the freedom of the press protected by the Virginia Declaration of Rights would permit someone to claim the freedom of the press as an escape from otherwise legitimate contractual liability. A similar point could be made about fraud, extortion, and many other wrongs the carrying out of which necessarily require the use of written or spoken words.[4]

The examples just provided are of course rather extreme, but the message is nonetheless important. There is nothing talismanic about the use of a printing press, or the use of words, or the use of a typewriter such that these particular methods of acting automatically give the actor immunity from governmental sanction. Rather, it is only speaking, writing, or printing of a certain variety that triggers the stringent protection that Mason properly characterized in the Virginia Declaration as "one of the greatest bulwarks of liberty."

What, then, is it that freedom of speech and freedom of the press are concerned with, if it is something less than the totality of verbal, written, or printed conduct? One way of answering this question would be to consult history, and in doing so we can see that it is likely that Mason had some rather specific ideas in mind. We know, for example, that he was personally familiar with the writings of John Trenchard and Thomas Gordon, published anonymously in England in the first half of the eighteenth century under the pseudonym "Cato," and reprinted in almost every colonial newspaper.[5] Indeed, the specific "bulwark of liberty" language, contained not only in the Virginia Declaration of Rights, but also in a Resolution of the Massachusetts House eight years earlier, comes directly from *Cato's Letters*.[6] We know also that Mason had access to and read the similarly anonymous "Letters of Junius."[7] And we know that Mason was a reader of the writings of the English dissident John Wilkes, and had even organized efforts on behalf of Wilkes when Wilkes ran afoul of official displeasure in England.[8]

The writings of Cato, of Junius, and of Wilkes all stressed the importance of freedom of the press. But what is especially interesting in this context is that all of these writings focused on a particular reason for treating freedom of speech and freedom of the press as so vitally important. By less than elaborate historical reconstruction one can therefore surmise that Mason was influenced and inspired by this particular conception and justification of freedom of the press, and that justifies us in giving it especially close scrutiny.

The arguments of Cato, Junius, and Wilkes are importantly distinct from the more familiar cornerstones of free speech theory. A century before Mason's time, John Milton, in the *Areopagitica*, and to a lesser extent John Locke, in his *Letters Concerning Toleration*, had argued for freedom of speech and press in terms of the search for truth.[9] They relied on the proposition, seemingly tenuous now but accepted by the naive faith of the Enlightenment, that truth would invariably prevail in its battle with falsehood if only the two are allowed to confront each other unencumbered by government restrictions. And their arguments were the intellectual precursors of the "marketplace of ideas" concepts that have long been staples of American legal free speech ideology.[10]

In contrast to these arguments premised on the search for truth, Cato, Junius, and Wilkes relied in large part on the particular nature of democratic theory. They assumed that it is the function of government to act in accordance with the wishes and best interests of the people. But they had noticed from observation, and Wilkes knew from personal experience, that governments do not always act in accordance with the interests of the people. Governments, after all, are not abstract entities. They are composed of governors, human beings possessed not only with human strengths, but also with human failings, including bias, prejudice, greed, and selfishness. As a result of these human weaknesses, it becomes quite likely that the interests of the governors as people, concerned with protecting their own power, prerogatives, and interests, will diverge from the interests and responsibilities of the governors as trustees of government, charged with acting solely in the best interests of the public. As a result, it is seen as necessary that there be some check on the potential excesses of the fallible human beings of government. To Cato, Junius, and Wilkes, as well as to Spinoza and Hume, freedom of speech and freedom of the press constituted the most important check of all.[11] Cato, for example, argued that if our rulers were publicly examined and criticized, then they would be less likely to take actions that were not in the best interests of the people. But if their actions were not subject to public scrutiny, then there would be little to prevent the rulers from acting in their own rather than the public's interest. "The exposing therefore of publick Wickedness, as it is a Duty which every Man owes to Truth and his Country, can never be a Libel in the Nature of Things."[12]

Mason's inspiration, therefore, came not from a commitment to freedom of speech and press as a component of individual liberty or personal freedom. Nor did it come from a faith in an open marketplace of ideas as the best test of truth in any field of inquiry. Rather, it came from a profound distrust of excess governmental power, especially as that power related to the very functioning of government itself. In order to guard against the evils that might flow from this excess governmental power, it was necessary to have a check, and freedom of speech and press was seen as ideally suited to perform this "checking function."[13]

This view suggests that not all speaking or writing is to be protected, but only those communications that may in some way contribute to the process of restraining the excesses of government. It would seem, therefore, that speaking or writing about the governmental or political process, or about public officials in general, is what "the" freedom of speech and press is all about. To some extent that may be an oversimplification. We cannot be sure whether Mason and his contemporaries viewed the political and governmental as the exclusive domain of freedom of speech and press. It is clear, however, that they considered it to be at the core.[14]

II

The title of this address promised an inquiry that was in some way philosophical, but thus far the mode has been primarily historical. It is now time to shift away from the historical mode, but it is necessary to explain first why, to me at least, this shift is necessary.

I suggested above that the words of the Virginia Declaration of Rights, as well as the words of the First Amendment to the Constitution of the United States, are, although undoubtedly strong, hardly self-defining. These particular words share the generality and abstraction of the documents of which they are a part. I do not mean this as a criticism. Abstract documents such as the Virginia Declaration of Rights and the United States Constitution are highly inspirational, and have demonstrated as well that their very abstraction enables them to stand the test of time. But this abstraction, so vital to the long term survival of constitutions and the societies built around them, is likely to be of little comfort to the conscientious legislator seeking guidance, or to the judge who must adjudicate a concrete controversy at a particular point in time. For those whose official position or function requires more specific direction of what the law mandates, the detailed complexity of the Internal Revenue Code is far more reassuring then the vague generalities of the Constitution.

In the face of this indeterminacy of many of the most important and frequently litigated constitutional provisions—freedom of speech and press, equal protection of the laws, due process of law, unreasonable searches and seizures, cruel and unusual punishment, free exercise of religion, and many others—much of the common wisdom has it that we should look to the original intent of the drafters.[15] Under this view, when the text does not by the plain meaning of its terms provide the answers to the questions that now confront us, we must attempt to discover what was intended by those who can claim authorship of the text. Thus, if it can be shown that James Madison was the primary drafter of the First Amendment, and if it can be shown, as is the case, that Madison was directly inspired by the language in the Virginia Declaration of Rights, then the specific purposes of the latter provision, as imagined in 1776, should at least be relevant to and should perhaps even control the current disposition of cases arising before the courts that require interpretation of the First Amendment.[16]

The foregoing statement of the "intentionalist" position is admittedly an oversimplification, but there can be no doubt that the basic idea remains pervasive. If we are in doubt about a question of constitutional interpretation, we should consult and try to remain faithful to the intentions of the framers. To do anything else is to encourage judicial tyranny.

But such a view, popular as it may be, seems almost insulting to men like Mason and Madison. Although neither had the practical lawyering experience of a John Marshall, for example, they were men of affairs and men of the world, and thus were undoubtedly familiar with a wide range of legal documents. They were well aware of detail and precision in draftsmanship, and it makes no sense to doubt that they had the ability and the exposure to have drafted documents much longer and much more detailed than either the Virginia Declaration of Rights or the United States Constitution. But they and their contemporaries did not do so, choosing instead to draft documents that bore no resemblance to formal, detailed, and technical legal documents.

It is at least bizarre to suppose that the particular style of the United States Constitution, with all of its majestic generality, is attributable to a collective oversight the likes of which history has never seen. Rather, we must assume at the very least that general language was used intentionally. And if people who know how to write in specifics chose instead to write in generalities, the only sensible explanation is that those who had the vision to draft documents such as these did not wish (and therefore did not *intend*) future generations to be bound to the specific conceptions, problems, and solutions that the framers had in mind in 1776 or 1791.[17] Unless we wish to treat the framers, and the ratifying conventions or state legislatures as well, as either negligent, reckless, or just plain stupid, then we must assume that general language was employed for the very purpose of allowing future generations to apply certain broad principles to the specific problems of their own generations, and not be forced to rewrite or ignore fundamental constitutive documents whenever new issues presented themselves.

But even the perspective just described seems a bit strange, because it is still in an important sense tethered to original intent, albeit at a much higher level of abstraction. For if we look at much of the rest of law, we see that the words of a legal document have a primacy and an authoritativeness of their own, purely by virtue of the adoption or enactment of those words.[18] A contract is to be interpreted according to the reasonable meaning of the words of that contract, regardless of the subjective intent of the contracting parties.[19] Language is deemed defamatory with reference to the plain meaning of the words used, and it is no defense that the speaker did not intend for the words to be given a defamatory interpretation.[20] And in interpreting statutes, the general rule is that the clear words of the statute are conclusive, rendering recourse to legislative intent not only unnecessary but in general impermissible, at least when the effect would be the rejection of the clear import of the language as written.[21] We write down our laws, just as we write down our contracts, for the very purpose of making the written form authoritative, and thus it is in the nature of law that the inquiry not only begins but in an important way ends with the particular verbal form that emerges as the authoritative document.

This approach, when applied to interpretation of the Constitution, creates little problem when we are dealing with quite specific provisions, such as the requirement that the President be at least 35 years of age, or the requirement that a jury trial be granted in any common law case involving at least 20 dollars. But things become substantially more difficult when we are dealing with the great abstractions of the Constitution,[22] including the freedom of speech, press, and religion, the prohibition of unreasonable searches and seizures, the impermissibility of cruel and unusual punishments, and the requirements of due process and equal protection of the laws. It is with reference to these quite abstract provisions that the backward pull towards original intent is greatest, because the search for specific historical events that have already occurred seemingly provides a source of certainty in a sea of abstractions.[23]

In many instances, the certainty of history is little more than an illusion. Documents and records are usually incomplete and subject to the perceptions and biases of their creators, and the contemporary search for historical evidence is inevitably distorted by the tendency to look only for what we wish to find, making the inquiry invariably value-laden. All of this is especially true with respect to searching for the intentions of the framers of the Constitution, where all too often it appears, as with Antonio's view of the use of Scripture,[24] that there is always some fragment of constitutional history available to support the particular interpretation that is being urged.

The vagaries of constitutional history and original intent are particularly apparent with respect to the First Amendment. There is little evidence that the drafters did much thinking about particulars, and it is likely that they had little more than the general idea that freedom of speech and freedom of the press were good things that were worthy of constitutional protection.[25] But my thesis does not depend on the lack of historical evidence, and would be the same even if the intentions of the framers with respect to the First Amendment, or any other constitutional provision, could be ascertained with certainty. For even if we could know exactly what took place in the minds of Mason, Madison, and their contemporaries, and even if we could put aside the point that it was not their thoughts but their specific words, and those words alone, that were ratified by the states,[26] it still remains the case that the words themselves, by the very fact of appearing in a plainly legal document,[27] are authoritative in and of themselves. And if this is the case, then it is plainly permissible for the courts, charged with the task of interpreting the Constitution,[28] to interpret those generalities by working out theories of what those words can mean *now*. This does not mean that judges are precluded from looking at history, but it does mean that history occupies no special pride of place among the battery of tools available for constitutional interpretation. The fact that the words of a constitutional provision stand by themselves as part of an authoritative document means that judges are by no means required to look at history, and they are certainly not required to look at history alone to the exclusion of any other source of enlightenment on how best to interpret the vague clauses of the Constitution. It is both expected and legitimate that judges will work out theories of what, for example, freedom of speech and freedom of the press should mean now, and it is likely and unimpeachable that this inquiry will be every bit as much philosophical as it is historical.

III

Following the mandate I have just outlined, it therefore seems incumbent on us to attempt to work out the philosophical roots of the concept of freedom of speech and press. And I do not use the word "roots" in a temporal sense, because we need not and should not engage in an exercise in the history of ideas, but rather an exercise in philosophical and policy analysis now, albeit one that will gradually evolve over time as a store of precedents is developed. To deny that we are bound by history is by no means to deny that we can learn from it.

If we look at the problem of free speech as a philosophical question, we can be said to be searching for a reason, or reasons why freedom of speech and press is specially important, such as to justify specific constitutional protection. It is not enough to assert simply that freedom to speak and to write is a good thing, for there are many good things that were not deemed sufficiently important to mandate constitutional protection.[29] A serious philosophical inquiry into the question of freedom of speech, especially in the American constitutional context, must seek to justify treating speaking and writing as so important that they must be protected by means other than those we normally consider sufficient to protect other important aspects of our liberty.

One leading candidate for such a philosophical justification is the notion of a search for truth, a view that has dominated free speech ideology from Milton to Jefferson to John Stuart Mill to Oliver Wendell Holmes to the present day.[30] All have argued, in one form or another, that truth has some inherent power to prevail in the competition among ideas. As a result, governmental selection among ideas invariably produces more harm than good, and we are better off if we rely on the free marketplace of ideas rather than on any form of governmental intervention in the search for truth.

These ideals sound grand as high theory, but one must wonder whether they have survived the test of history. Put quite starkly, truth does not always win out. Falsity, for reasons of bias, prejudice, superstition, and plain ignorance, often has a surprising degree of not only strength, but also endurance. The inherent power of truth and reason was one of the faiths of the Enlightenment, but more contemporary psychological and sociological insights have confirmed the judgment of history that truth is often the loser in its battle with falsity.

Of course it is not necessary to believe that truth always wins out in its battle with error in order to subscribe to some version of the theory of the marketplace of ideas. This epistemological argument for freedom of speech and press could still be accepted by resorting merely to an argument from relative incompetence.[31] That is, no matter how bad the public might be at separating truth from error, government has shown itself to be even worse. Given that we can never eliminate completely the acceptance of error and the rejection of truth, we must then pick the long-run strategy that will maximize our knowledge. And from this perspective, it is argued, government has shown itself to be so poor an assessor of truth that we are far better off relying on the open marketplace of ideas, despite its imperfections.

But in many areas of knowledge even this more attenuated version of the "argument from truth" seems at odds with our common perceptions. We are quite comfortable with the proposition that the Securities and Exchange Commission is better able to determine truth within its area of expertise than is the average investor in securities, and similar presuppositions underlay such other governmental agencies as the Federal Trade Commission, with respect to product advertising, and the Food and Drug Administration, in its dealings regarding the labels and ingredients of foods and drugs. In many other areas I would be quite satisfied to accept governmental selection among propositions if the alternative were some sort of epistemological majority rule.

In other areas, however, we properly distrust government's ability objectively to sort out truth from falsity. In general this distrust is prompted by the particular biases of government. Thus, we can hardly expect government disinterestedly to determine the truth of criticism of that very government or its officials.[32] Nor can we expect government to be objective in its evaluation of the merits or potential dangers of a wide range of political, moral, social, and similar controversies, because we elect governments on the basis of those governments' holding particular positions on these issues. To the extent that those views are challenged, the particular positions of the governors are in jeopardy, and it is again difficult to expect objectivity under these circumstances.

Many theorists, most prominently Alexander Meiklejohn, have argued that freedom of speech is an adjunct to that formulation of democracy that emphasizes democracy as embodying total sovereignty of the people at large.[33] If the people are masters and elected officials their servants, Meiklejohn argued, then it would be anomalous to permit the servants to preselect the information that is available to the masters. Yet this, he maintained, is precisely what happens when governmental officials can exercise any control whatsoever over the information and arguments that may reach the public at large.

This is a powerful argument, and it has influenced much recent constitutional law interpreting the First Amendment,[34] but the premises of the argument seem questionable upon closer scrutiny.[35] For if the argument is premised on the notion of popular sovereignty, then presumably ultimate power to do anything resides with the people at large, and no decision is beyond popular control. Yet if this is the case, then what in the argument from democracy prevents the people themselves, in the exercise of their sovereign power, from deciding that certain ideas and information are too wrong or too dangerous to be allowed wide circulation? Similarly, there seems nothing in the argument that would prohibit the people, again in the exercise of their assumed sovereign powers, from delegating to certain officials the authority to determine what information might be too harmful for the people to receive, and to exercise a power of censorship accordingly.

The argument has also been presented that freedom of speech and freedom of the press are important components of individuality, in the sense that these freedoms aid in personal self-development, self-expression, self-realization, or self-fulfillment, to take a sample of characterizations currently employed.[36] There seems little doubt that freedom of speech and press does lead to all of these things, but that conclusion is insufficient to justify the conclusion that they are deserving of special and distinct political, legal, and constitutional protection.[37] For the values of self-development, self-realization, and the like can also be served by many other conditions. For example, world travel, the choice of one's companions, interesting employment, and one's style of appearance may also be forms of self-expression, and may also be of great assistance in self-fulfillment, yet we properly do not treat these as of the same order as freedom of speech and press. Here the problem is not that the argument from individuality does not prove enough, but that it proves too much. For if the principle of freedom of speech is premised on the undeniable virtues of individuality, then the principle of free speech collapses into a principle of general liberty. Liberty is of course a good thing, but in exploring the question of freedom of speech we are searching for some reason why speech and press should be treated *specially.* Our task is to look for a justification that compels or at least permits us to protect speech and press *even more* than we protect liberty in general. The problem with the argument from individuality is that it is seen, upon closer analysis, to apply with equal force to every form of self-expression or to every source of self-fulfillment. The argument, therefore, is nothing more than an argument for the general advantages of personal liberty. And an argument only for personal liberty cannot provide the justification we are seeking for the creation of a right of special importance and special strength.

This survey of possible philosophical bases for the principles of freedom of speech and freedom of the press has been of necessity somewhat abbreviated. But this truncated version of arguments I have made at much greater length elsewhere is presented here to demonstrate two important points. First, that many of the standard arguments for freedom of speech and press cannot withstand close scrutiny, and thus it is important to reexamine many of the tired and traditional platitudes about freedom of speech and freedom of the press. Second, and of particular importance here, is that all of the valid arguments seem to have something special to do with a particular distrust of governmental power. Because of the biases, prejudices, and selfishness of the fallible human beings who hold high political office and the power that accompanies it, those individuals are likely to be less capable of evenhandedly regulating activities that threaten those positions than they are able to regulate those activities that do not constitute such an immediate personal threat. And if we were to compile a catalogue of those activities that would constitute such a threat to the power, prestige, and position of those who hold high (or even low) political office, high on the list would be criticism or other threatening discussion of the policies and personal qualifications of those in power. It thus seems likely that we can make a philosophical—policy—empirical—behavioral argument that centers around the particular suspicion of governmental power to deal with certain forms of speaking and writing—those forms that in some way, even remotely, relate to the governmental process.

This argument that grounds freedom of speech and freedom of the press in a particular distrust of governmental officials to deal with a certain kind of communication may not be the only argument for freedom of speech and press. All too often we assume that a principle that has one name must therefore have one simple essence or unifying feature.[39] But that is an unjustified assumption, as much in talking about freedom of speech as in talking about anything else. There is no reason to suppose that freedom of speech and press must necessarily be one and only one principle, and it is quite likely that we are dealing with a collection of different principles that happen to be joined under the particular simplifying rubric that happens to be found in our most fundamental documents. Still, however, the argument from the distrust of the excesses of governmental power seems the most powerful of the many arguments that can be made for freedom of speech and press, and it is also the argument that is most able to explain the special position we grant to freedom of speech and press in our system of government and constitutional protection.

IV

It is noteworthy that the foregoing investigation—partly philosophical, partly psychological, partly political, partly sociological—has generated a conclusion strikingly similar to that produced by the historical analysis presented earlier. The argument I have just offered seems to put some empirical and philosophical flesh on the barebones suggestions made far more eloquently by Cato, Junius, and Wilkes, and then embodied into fundamental law by George Mason and his contemporaries. Although naturally expressed more in the language of passionate and troubled times than in the language of dispassionate philosophical analysis, the ideas developed at the spawning of this nation have once again shown themselves to be the product of minds of great depth as well as of great vision.

In this connection, it is worthwhile to focus again on the fact that freedom of speech and freedom of the press were set forth in 1776 and then in 1791 (as well as in most other state constitutions of the new nation)[40] as part of controlling legal documents. As we now know, of course, the decision to do so was a decision of great importance, and the source of most of the greatness and longevity of the United States Constitution. But it also calls into question the common assumption that Mason and his contemporaries were demanding nothing more than their rights as Englishmen.[41] For although the English, then and now, have placed great stock in the values of freedom of speech and freedom of the press,[42] they have yet to establish a mechanism, and certainly did not have one then, to protect these rights *against* the acts of a sovereign, whether that sovereign be a king, a legislature, or even the public in general. Legal control of the sovereign suggests legal authority above the sovereign power, and this notion of legally limited sovereignty is alien to the English constitutional framework.[43]

But once we recognize that to Cato, to Junius, to Wilkes, to Mason, and to Madison freedom of speech and freedom of the press were checks against the excesses of self-interested governors, many of whom would hold legislative rather than executive positions, then it becomes anomalous to suggest that the "rights of Englishmen" can be protected in the English style. To protect rights against the government by making that government itself the primary enforcer and protector of those rights suggests at the least conflict of interest and quite likely pure folly.[44] It is like asking the home team not only to provide the baseballs, but also to call balls and strikes.

Although judicial review as we now know it may not have been finally settled until the Supreme Court's decision in *Marbury* v. *Madison*,[45] the American approach to freedom of speech and press, and to individual rights in general, constituted a substantial departure from the English model even without the institution of judical review. For the very decision to put the protection of rights against the government in a document intended to bind that very government absolutely represents an approach totally different from that employed then and now in England.[46] It may be that Mason, Madison, and others were at one level doing nothing more than fighting for their rights as Englishmen. But at a different level, the fact that these rights were embodied in legal documents intended to be binding and authoritative shows that they were highly sensitive to the fact that they, as Englishmen, had been forced to take up arms in order to preserve these rights against government. By choosing to entrust the enforcement of these rights not to legislatures, and not to the executive, and not to soldiers at Lexington, Concord, Saratoga, Valley Forge, and Yorktown, but rather to law as enforced by an independent judiciary, Mason and others made a decision that has largely been responsible for the stability of the nation.

V

It seems appropriate to conclude by returning once again to the present. Whether the inquiry be historical or philosophical, it is undoubtedly important now to explore the philosophical roots of the principles of freedom of speech and freedom of the press. Thirty years ago almost every free speech case concerned the extent of free speech rights of political dissidents, such as socialists, communists, syndicalists, anarchists, and related other "ists."[47] We may have been troubled or divided by how much free speech protection ought to be granted to such people, but there was no question that the suppression of their activities at least created free speech issues. Because there was this core of agreement about the kinds of activities that triggered a First Amendment inquiry, the need to explore the philosophical underpinnings of the First Amendment was considerably less pressing.

Now, however, the First Amendment has become, as the result of judicial action, much broader. Unlike the situation of times past, the First Amendment is now at least implicated in governmental action regarding commercial advertising,[48] regulation of campaign financing,[49] libel and slander,[50] obscenity,[51] and many other areas previously considered to be well outside the coverage of the First Amendment. Where are we to stop? Have we gone too far? We can answer these questions only if we have some conception of the purposes of the First

Amendment. For what is inside the First Amendment and what is outside the First Amendment cannot, as I said at the outset of this address, be determined merely by looking at the words of the constitutional text. No amount of staring at the words "the freedom of speech, or of the press" will help courts to answer questions such as the one recently presented in the District of Columbia of whether sleeping in the park as a form of protest is an activity protected by the First Amendment against governmental interference.[52] In order to decide cases like this, we have to search for the foundations of the First Amendment, and then determine if the novel case at hand has anything to do with the reasons for having the First Amendment at all. As I have argued earlier, it is my view that this inquiry should be primarily philosophical rather than historical. But the fact that in this case the philosophical and historical inquiries led to more or less the same place should show us that, even when we are engaging in a philosophical investigation, we should know that we ignore the wisdom and insights of men like George Mason only at our peril.

Notes

1. Virginia Declaration of Rights No. 12 (1776). Virtually identical language was subsequently used by North Carolina. North Carolina Declaration of Rights No. XV (1776).

2. "Congress shall make no law . . . abridging the freedom of speech, or of the press; . . ." United States Constitution, amendment I (1791).

3. For more extensive parsing of the particular words of the First Amendment, see Melville Nimmer, "The Right to Speak from *Times* to *Time:* First Amendment Theory Applied to Libel and Misapplied to Privacy," 56 *California Law Review* 935 (1968); Frederick Schauer, "Categories and the First Amendment: A Play in Three Acts," 34 *Vanderbilt Law Review* 265 (1981); William Van Alstyne, "A Graphic Review of the Free Speech Clause," 70 *California Law Review* 107 (1982).

4. For an expanded discussion of this point, see Frederick Schauer, "Speech and 'Speech'—Obscenity and 'Obscenity': An Exercise in the Interpretation of Constitutional Language," 67 *Georgetown Law Journal* 899 (1979).

5. Robert A. Rutland, ed., *The Papers of George Mason*, 3 vols. (Chapel Hill, North Carolina: University of North Carolina Press, 1970), 1:73, 193, 279–81. On Cato's influence on American free speech doctrine in general, see David Anderson, "The Origins of the Press Clause," 30 *UCLA Law Review* 455 (1983); Vincent Blasi, "The Checking Value in First Amendment Theory," *American Bar Foundation Research Journal* 521 (1977).

6. [John Trenchard and Thomas Gordon], *Cato's Letters, or, Essays on Liberty, Civil and Religious, and Other Important Subjects* (London: W. Wilkins, et. al., 1737), Essay No. 15. For the text and description of the Massachusetts resolution, see Leonard Levy, *Legacy of Suppression* (Cambridge, Massachusetts: Harvard University Press, 1960), 69.

7. *The Papers of George Mason*, 1:125, 232.

8. *The Papers of George Mason*, 1:129, 290.

9. These and related arguments are discussed at length in Frederick Schauer, *Free Speech: A Philosophical Enquiry* (Cambridge: Cambridge University Press, 1982), Chapter 2.

10. See, for example, Abrams v. United States, 2SO U.S. 616, 630–31 (1919) (Holmes, J., dissenting); Whitney v. California, 274 U.S. 357, 375–78 (1927) (Brandeis, J., concurring); Dennis v. United States, 341 U.S. 494, 546–53 (1951) (Frankfurter, J., concurring); International Brotherhood of Electrical Workers v. NLRB, 181 F.2d 3 (2d Cir. 1950) (L. Hand, J.).

11. On the contributions of Spinoza and Hume to free speech theory, see Frederick Schauer, "Free Speech and the Argument from Democracy," in *Liberal Democracy* (NOMOS XXV), ed. J. Roland Pennock and John Chapman (New York: New York University Press, 1983), 241.

12. *Cato's Letters*, Essay No. 32, quoted in Anderson, "The Origin of the Press Clause," 525.

13. See Blasi, "Checking Value."

14. Taking political values to be at the core of the protection of freedom of speech and freedom of the press need not preclude the inclusion of speech that is not explicitly political. See Harry Kalven, "The *New York Times* Case: A Note on the 'Central Meaning of the

First Amendment'," *The Supreme Court Review* (1964): 191; Alexander Meiklejohn, "The First Amendment is an Absolute," *The Supreme Court Review* (1961) 245.

15. Intentionalist theories in constitutionalist interpretation vary with the extent to which they would follow the very specific instances imagined by the framers. The most extreme version of intentionalism is found in Raoul Berger, *Government By Judiciary: The Transformation of the Fourteenth Amendment* (Cambridge, Massachusetts: Harvard University Press, 1977). For a much more plausible version, see Henry Monaghan, "Our Perfect Constitution," 56 *New York University Law Review* 353 (1981).

16. I am in this context leaving alone the question of whose intent is relevant. But we must not forget that in reference to the United States Constitution the relevant legal document must be ratified by the states, making the question of intent much more complicated.

17. For articulations of this weak intentionalist position, see, for example, Ronald Dworkin, *Taking Rights Seriously* (Cambridge, Massachusetts: Harvard University Press, 1977), 131–49; Laurence Tribe, *American Constitutional Law* (Mineola, New York: The Foundation Press, 1978), Chapter 3.

18. What follows is an abbreviated version of an argument made in Frederick Schauer, "An Essay on Constitutional Language," 29 *UCLA Law Review* 797 (1982).

19. Hotchkiss v. National City Bank of New York, 200 F.287 (S.D.N.Y. 1911); Ricketts v. Pennsylvania Ry. Co., 153 F.2d 757 (2d Cir. 1946); Smith v. Hughes, 6 Q.B. 597 (1871).

20. Lyman v. New England Newspaper Pub. Co., 286 Mass. 258, 190 N.E. 542 (1934); Roberts v. Camden, 103 Eng. Rep. 508 (K.B. 1807).

21. See generally Note, "Intent, Clear Statements, and the Common Law: Statutory Interpretation in the Supreme Court," 95 *Harvard Law Review* 892 (1982).

22. Among the most prominent characterizations is Justice Jackson's reference to the "great silences of the Constitution." H. P. Hood & Sons, Inc. v. DuMond, 336 U.S. 525, 535 (1949).

23. See William Rehnquist, "The Notion of a Living Constitution," 54 *Texas Law Review* 693 (1976).

24. "Mark you this Bassanio, / The Devil can cite Scripture for his

purpose." William Shakespeare, *The Merchant of Venice*, Act I, scene 2, lines 98–99.

25. See Thomas Kauper, review of *Political Freedom*, by Alexander Meiklejohn, 58 *Michigan Law Review* 619 (1960).

26. "Nothing but the text itself was adopted by the people." Joseph Story, *Commentaries on the Constitution of the United States*, Fourth Edition (Boston, 1873), 300.

27. In a way the statement in the text is question-begging, for the extent to which any constitution, and particularly the Constitution of the United States, is like any other legal document is in one sense the very question to be answered. If it is a political rather than legal document, or if it is in some other way *sui generis*, then the precise nature of the relationship between text and intent may differ. Dealing with these issues is part of a work I currently have in progress.

28. I am assuming the legitimacy of Marbury v. Madison, 1 Cranch (5 U.S.) 137 (1803). Again, however, this is by no means a clear-cut proposition. See generally William Van Alstyne, "A Critical Guide to Marbury v. Madison," *Duke Law Journal* (1969), 1.

29. We should not forget that to a great extent our most basic needs of food, shelter, and personal safety are not protected by the Constitution.

30. See Frederick Schauer, *Free Speech*, for a critical analysis in depth of this "argument from truth."

31. Ibid. Chapter 2.

32. This has been accepted as the mandate for making it virtually impossible for public officials to recover damages for libel and slander. See New York Times Co. v. Sullivan, 376 U.S. 254 (1964); Garrison v. Louisiana, 379 U.S. 64 (1964).

33. Alexander Meiklejohn, *Political Freedom: The Constitutional Powers of the People* (New York: Oxford University Press, 1965); Frank Morrow, "Speech, Expression, and the Constitution," *Ethics* 85 (1975): 235.

34. See William Brennan, "The Supreme Court and the Meiklejohn Interpretation of the First Amendment," 79 *Harvard Law Review* 1 (1965).

35. For a more extensive discussion, see Frederick Schauer, "Free Speech and the Argument from Democracy."

36. See Edwin Baker, "Scope of the First Amendment Freedom of Speech," 25 *UCLA Law Review* 964 (1978); Martin Redish, "The

Value of Free Speech," 130 *University of Pennsylvania Law Review* 591 (1982); David A. J. Richards, "Free Speech and Obscenity Law: Toward a Moral Theory of the First Amendment," 123 *University of Pennsylvania Law Review* 45 (1974).

37. An expanded version of the argument is in Frederick Schauer, *Free Speech,* Chapters 1, 4, and 5.

38. In Frederick Schauer, *Free Speech,* I present these arguments totally divorced from the American political or constitutional context. The presence of the First Amendment, of course, directs and constrains the argument in the American context in a way that it does not if we are considering a purely abstract question of political and social philosophy.

39. The reaction against essentialism is one of the most prominent features of contemporary analytic philosophy. The guiding influence here is Ludwig Wittgenstein, *Philosophical Investigations* (G.E.M. Anscombe trans.) (Oxford: Basil Blackwell, 1953). The Wittgensteinian notion of a "family resemblance" seems quite appropriate for the several principles subsumed under the heading "freedom of speech," among them, perhaps, a check on the excesses of government, open inquiry in the sciences and other academic disciplines, and an aversion to censorship of art or literature.

40. See generally Anderson, "The Origins of the Press Clause," which sets forth the various provisions.

41. See Helen Hill, *George Mason, Constitutionalist* (Gloucester, Massachusetts: Peter Smith, 1966).

42. See, for example, A. V. Dicey, *Introduction to the Study of the Law of the Constitution,* 9th ed., Edited by E. C. S. Wade (London: Macmillan, 1952), Chapter 6.

43. Ibid., Chapters 1–3.

44. See Ronald Dworkin, *Taking Rights Seriously,* Chapters 5–7.

45. 1 Cranch (5 U.S.) 137 (1803).

46. Dicey, Chapters 1–3.

47. Most of the landmark free speech cases fit this characterization. Among the more prominent examples are Schenck v. United States, 249 U.S. 47 (1919); Debs v. United States, 249 U.S. 211 (1919); Abrams v. United States, 250 U.S. 616 (1919); Gitlow v. New York, 268 U.S. 652 (1925); Whitney v. California, 274 U.S. 357 (1927); Fiske v. Kansas, 274 U.S. 380 (1927); Dennis v. United States, 341 U.S. 494 (1951).

48. Virginia Pharmacy Board v. Virginia Consumer Council, 425

U.S.748 (1976); Linmark Associates, Inc. v. Township of Willingboro, 431 U.S. 85 (1977); Central Hudson Gas v. Public Service Commission, 100 S. Ct. 2343 (1980).

49. Buckley v. Valeo, 424 U.S. 1 (1976).

50. New York Times Co. v. Sullivan, 376 U.S. 254 (1964); Gertz v. Robert Welch, Inc., 418 U.S. 323 (1974).

51. Roth v. United States, 354 U.S. (1957); Miller v. California, 413 U.S. 15 (1973); Paris Adult Theatre I v. Slaton, 413 U.S. 49 (1973); Jenkins v. Georgia, 418 U.S. 153 (1974).

52. Community for Creative Non-Violence v. Watt, 703 F.2d 586 (D.C. Cir. 1983). A sharply divided Court of Appeals upheld the First Amendment rights of the sleepers.

4

American Foreign Policy and Human Rights: The New Realism

CHARLES WILLIAM MAYNES
Editor, *Foreign Policy*

> A large part of history is . . . replete with the struggle for . . . human rights, an eternal struggle in which a final victory can never be won. But to tire in that struggle would mean the ruin of society.
>
> —Albert Einstein[1]

IN EINSTEIN'S WORDS LIES A TRUTH THAT CAN INFORM THE LARGER national debate in the United States over the role that human rights should play in United States foreign policy. For there is in that debate often a level of intolerance that Einstein's wisdom about the unending nature of the struggle could help to reduce.

The intolerance, although regrettable, is understandable. If one man opposes another's point of view on, say, the appropriate level of social security payments, the first may conclude that the second is wrong but he does not charge the second with being wicked, immoral, or villainous. The second man may have a mistake on his hands but he does not have blood on his hands.

Consider now disagreements over human rights policy. If one man believes that another is preventing the first from enjoying rights that our own Declaration of Independence says are "inalienable," then the charge may not only be that one's opponent has committed a political mistake but that he has transgressed the sacred laws of the land, of nature, or even of God. Another man's position then becomes not a mistake but an abomination that must be ended almost at any cost.

Einstein, however, recognized not only the centrality of the struggle for human rights, but also the impermanence of any victory. That knowledge should both steel one for future struggles and prepare one for temporary setbacks. I hope, therefore, that in approaching this discussion we can recognize that while some men are wicked, the problem usually is that most are not sufficiently wise, and that what we are seeking in our discussion is not condemnation of others but clarification for ourselves.

We are here tonight to honor the memory of an American statesman, George Mason, who himself understood that if victory in politics and human rights is never final and that if there is always the need to strive for yet another victory to preserve central gains, victory comes easier if society is protected by a framework of laws that favors freedom and not authority.

George Mason is, in effect, the father of the First Amendment, which is the ultimate guarantee of all American rights. As we all know, that amendment states: "Congress shall make no law respecting an establishment of religion, or prohibiting the free exercise thereof; or abridging the freedom of speech, or of the press; or the right of the people peaceably to assemble, and to petition the Government for a redress of grievances."

As the editor of a public policy journal, I have a special attachment to that amendment. Nevertheless, Mason's revolutionary step was not in working to ensure that America would be a land of religious freedom or of a free press but in reversing, in writing and in a supreme governmental document, the traditional relationship between citizen and state. Throughout history it had been the citizen who owed duties to the state, which in turn might bestow certain rights on the citizen. These rights, however, could be withdrawn. Mason argued that the state had to observe certain citizens' rights that could not be violated under any circumstances. Mason thus set the United States apart from past constitutional practice and established a concern for human rights as a distinguishing feature of American democracy.

In this paper I want to explore in more depth the way in which the American attitude toward human rights has evolved. How do we define human rights? Are we changing our definition? Should we? And, finally, how does an American polity promote human rights not just at home but abroad?

The Two Concepts of Liberty

Any modern discussion of human rights in the broadest sense has to confront the classic statement of the question in Isaiah Berlin's seminal essay entitled "Two Concepts of Liberty." In this essay Berlin, a brilliant Oxford philosopher, distinguishes between two major concepts of liberty that help to explain many of the political struggles of the 20th century. One concept Berlin labels negative freedom and the other positive freedom.

Negative freedom, he asserts, is negative in the sense suggested by the following question: "What is the area within which the subject—a person or group of persons—is or should be left to do or be what he is able to do or be, without interference by other persons?"[2] In this question philosophers detect the seeds of modern democracy.

Freedom in the positive sense, he suggests, is conveyed by this question: What, or who, is the source of control or interference that can determine someone to do, or be, this rather than that?[3] In this question philosophers detect the roots of modern totalitarianism.

It is generally accepted that the American historical tradition strongly favors the first concept of freedom. The less government the best government is a common American view, and it is a view fervently favored by the current administration in Washington, which, acting on this faith, has even proposed to sell part of the United States weather service to private industry. Historically, it is true that Americans have concentrated on limiting and constraining public authority rather than on increasing its positive obligations. The unique American attitude was quite clear after World War II during the drafting of the United Nations Universal Declaration of Human Rights. That document, as one might expect of a product of compromise, reflects both democratic emphasis on political rights and a socialist emphasis on economic rights. The United States, a leader in the effort to codify a system of international human rights obligations, accepted the compromise. Nevertheless, as United States delegate Eleanor Roosevelt, although socially progressive within our political system, stated at the time for the official United Nations record: ". . . [M]y government has made it clear in the course of the development of the declaration that it does not consider that the economic and social and cultural rights stated in the declaration imply an obligation on governments to assure the enjoyment of these rights by direct government action."

Why has the United States adopted that position? Americans, one might think, should want their people well-fed and employed as much as any other society. Why, then, have they generally followed the position articulated by Mrs. Roosevelt? There are probably two reasons: First, some conservative Americans oppose any suggestion that individuals have an inalienable claim on some body of economic rights because they believe that such a claim, if recognized as a right, will in effect require every government in the world to aspire to social democracy, and they strongly oppose such an aspiration for personal or ideological reasons. Second, other Americans maintain, in a pale reflection of Berlin's powerful arguments, that there is a fundamental difference between negative and positive rights. With the former, it is argued, a government need only stop certain actions, e.g., torture, and a citizen's rights will be automatically secured. In the case of the latter, a decision of a government to grant, say, economic rights to the citizen does not necessarily ensure that each individual in the land will enjoy those rights. President Carter stated publicly that every American had a human right to a job. But the Carter administration was not able to provide a job to every American. Reflecting on the apparent difference between negative and positive rights, some observers have argued that positive rights are not even human rights in the same sense as negative rights are human rights. For how can they be when it may be beyond a government's power to secure them?

Isaiah Berlin, as usual, is eloquent on the exact difference between negative political and positive economic rights:

> If the liberty of myself or my class or nation depends on the misery of a number of other human beings, the system which promotes this is unjust and immoral. But if I curtail or lose my freedom, in order to lessen the shame of such equality, and do not thereby materially increase the individual liberty of others,

> an absolute loss of liberty occurs. This may be compensated for by a gain in justice or in happiness or in peace but the loss remains, and it is a confusion of values to say that although my "liberal," individual freedom may go by the board, some other kind of freedom—"social" or "economic"—is increased.[4]

Lest one believe that the distinctions Berlin makes are of academic interest only, we can note that some foreign governments or their sympathizers employ precisely Berlin's distinction to explain away their lack of concern over other more egregious cases of human rights violations in either the political or economic field. Thus, right-wing commentators attempt to justify or explain away abuses of the human rights of blacks under apartheid on the grounds that South African blacks enjoy a higher standard of living than other black Africans and there is no assurance, given the general record in Africa, that a black government in South Africa would be able to create a climate equally favorable to economic progress. At the same time, left-wing commentators downplay abuses of the political rights of individuals or minorities in some Third World or communist states by arguing that the first priority is providing the majority with vital economic rights.

So a crucial question in the modern debate over human rights is whether the distinction between the negative and positive liberties remains as clear as Berlin implies in his classic essay. For his part, Berlin, himself gifted with humanity as well as brilliance, does acknowledge in his essay that "there are situations, as a nineteenth century Russian radical writer declared, in which boots are superior to the words of Shakespeare. For . . . the Egyptian peasant needs clothes or medicine before, and more than personal liberty."[5] But even in this concession Berlin is suggesting that the two spheres of freedom remain separate. Are there respects in which the two concepts of freedom are more alike than Berlin implies?

To answer that question, we need to clarify another distinction: that between equality of opportunity and equality of result. Most Americans, it is fair to say, support equality of opportunity for all individuals rather than equality of results for all individuals; and it is fear of the latter that most people have in mind when they state their opposition to the concept of economic and social rights as human rights.

Nevertheless, recognition that Americans by an overwhelming majority support equality of opportunity rather than equality of result does not in the end resolve very much; for that recognition overlooks the practical fact that the two are closely related. Without a certain minimum of equality of result in a society, it is questionable whether there can ever be equality of opportunity in that society. Without some guarantees of economic and social rights it becomes questionable whether certain political and civic rights can be exercised. Thus, First Amendment rights to a free press may not be terribly useful to a man who cannot read. Does this fact imply that the state therefore has a positive obligation to educate its citizenry so that they can exercise a negative right? Is education not only a human need but also a human right?

Or to press this issue further, negative rights are secured not in the orderly mind of a brilliant philosopher, but in the real world of political conflict and ethnic animosities. Is it possible for a state to secure the negative rights of its citizens unless it also does something positive to secure them? Berlin seems to assume that a state need only cease doing an evil act such as torture and the citizens' rights are automatically secured. But this statement assumes that the state is the only source of torture and that the state retains effective control of all governmental instruments.

Berlin's formulation, at bottom, rests on an assumption, in other words, about human nature that the events of the 20th century belie. That assumption is that if governments cease mistreating their citizens, the citizens themselves will cease mistreating one another. Perhaps citizens did act in this responsible way in the racially homogeneous country in which Berlin grew up. But now even England has lost much of its traditional civility and composure as a more racially diverse country has developed in the 20th century of porous borders and emigration from the poor South to the rich North.

So the reality is that modern governments do take positive actions to secure negative freedoms. How, then, is that different from positive actions to secure positive freedoms? It might be argued that a Federal court decision to strike down local laws barring blacks from the right to vote immediately enlarges the circle of freedom, whereas a law proclaiming the right of every American to a job does not create a single job. But given human ingenuity in avoiding unpleasant changes, the Federal court case does not necessarily enlarge the circle of freedom unless there is respectful local compliance. Further positive measures will be necessary. In like measure a law proclaiming the right to a job can be followed by an employment bill. In both cases measures of implementation are required to enlarge the circle of rights being enjoyed as opposed to being merely proclaimed.

At first, these philosophical comments may not seem immediately applicable to the real world of international human rights policy, but in fact the comments are directly relevant to some key dilemmas the United States faces in its effort to strengthen international respect for human rights.

A major debate within the United Nations is whether political or economic rights should enjoy priority. The developing countries, in asserting that priority should be given to economic rights, in effect take the position suggested by Berlin when he noted that the "Egyptian peasant needs clothes or medicine before, and more than personal liberty." How should a United States administration react to such a point of view? The Reagan and the Carter administrations have responded very differently to that question.

The Reagan-Carter Difference

The Carter administration reasoned that if its interest in human rights were to become a permanent feature of foreign policy not just in the United States but in other countries, America would have to work to institutionalize its international human rights campaign. But a fundamental problem was the developing countries' insistence on according priority to economic rights.

Reaching back to the wartime concerns of Franklin Delano Roosevelt and the Four Freedoms, of which one was "Freedom from Want," the Carter administration acknowledged, Eleanor Roosevelt's earlier statement to the United Nations notwithstanding, that human rights did embrace economic rights. The president signed not only the Covenant for Political and Civil Rights but also the Covenant for Economic and Social Rights. In the definitive speech in the Carter administration on the new human rights policy, Secretary of State Cyrus Vance advanced a hierarchy of rights: 1. rights of the integrity of the person (such as protection from murder, summary execution, torture, mistreatment); 2. certain socioeconomic rights which comprise basic needs (food, shelter, health care, and education); and 3. other civil and political rights.

The Vance list is interesting because it places civil and political rights in the third category or after socioeconomic rights. This decision did not betray a belief within the Carter administration that representative forms of government were less important than economic rights. It was more a concession to reality: an international consensus about the importance of the first two categories of rights was more likely to develop than one regarding the desirability of establishing in every government in the world an Anglo-Saxon system of representative government.

The Reagan administration takes a different position. It denies that economic rights are human rights. Regarding representative government it argues that political participation is not only an important right in itself, but also the best guarantee that other rights will be observed.[6]

Berlin, however, points out that the connection between civil rights and individual rights may not be as tight as Americans would assume. In particular, the negative sense of liberty involving the integrity of the person is, in Berlin's words, "not incompatible with some kinds of autocracy, or at any rate with the absence of self-government."[7] And indeed, as we know from periods of our history, a democracy may deprive some or all of its citizens of a great many liberties. Minorities in the United States have been denied certain basic rights throughout American history. Certain classes of Americans during periods of strain, such as the period when Senator Joseph McCarthy was at his height of power, have also lost some of their rights. Berlin points out that in contrast a liberal minded despot may allow his subjects a large measure of individual freedom.

Other nations have had a similar experience. From the standpoint of the citizens of some Third World countries, the metropolitan power during the era of colonialism was a despot, yet in the case of Britain or France or even Imperial Germany that power probably accorded the citizens of the colonized territories more individual freedom than they have enjoyed since they achieved the right to govern themselves. Nor is it true that democracies necessarily try harder than despotisms to secure the economic welfare of all of their citizens. Democracy can exist in the face of massive indifference to the unfair misery suffered by a significant minority of the population. True, that minority can never become a majority, or the government in a democratic system will be overthrown. But the economic deprivation of a minority within a democracy can be persistent, unfair, and humiliating from the standpoint of internationally accepted human rights.

The Carter administration attempted to square this circle by arguing that none of these rights should be neglected or forgotten. Thus, if in the interests of gaining an international consensus it made sense to concentrate on the rights inherent in the concept of the integrity of the person, this approach should not permit governments to argue that they could neglect their obligation under existing international covenants to work toward achievement of human rights in other areas.

In fact, however, the Carter administration did draw a distinction in practice, albeit not in rhetoric. In speeches before the United Nations, the United States might argue that it supported the covenant of economic and social rights as human rights, but the White House did not press ratification and in no case did the United States terminate aid because of a denial of economic rights. In addition, like the Reagan administration, the Carter administration in its annual survey for the Congress of human rights around the world, concentrated almost exclusively on political and civil rights. Moreover, as the United States Congress proved more and more resistant to adoption of the president's proposed aid program, the United States became more and more reluctant to contend that it was giving significant attention to economic and social rights as well as political and civil rights. For how could a country appear serious in such an assertion when it was so clearly moving in the other direction in the one program that offered the most tangible evidence of American concern with social and economic rights worldwide?

It can be argued, therefore, that in abandoning the position that economic rights are human rights, the Reagan administration only practiced euthanasia on an organism that was already near death. Thus it forthrightly restructured the annual report to the Congress to reflect its view that human rights were political and civil rights even though "programs which seek to eradicate poverty provide a crucial foundation for democratic political institutions." For that reason the annual report does include a section on economic and social circumstances.

Was this the right way to handle the problem? One way of looking at the matter is to say that if a nation cannot make its rhetoric consistent with its practice, then the best course is to change its rhetoric: the United States could acknowledge that the unique American contribution to the body of human rights has been its revolutionary role in creating political acceptance of the concept of negative rights. We are comfortable with the concept of negative rights; we are not comfortable with the concept of positive rights. We should therefore concentrate on the area that causes us the fewest domestic political problems and that raises the fewest philosophical concerns.

I believe this view is mistaken for several reasons. First, it assumes that human rights are forever fixed and that the American contribution to the establishment of the fixed body of human rights was the definitive contribution. This approach is hubristic and for that reason alone probably wrong. Second, this view reflects a very narrow reading of the history of this nation. It is true that in the American political tradition the founding fathers were determined through a series of checks and balances to prevent the central government from abusing its citizenry. But our founding fathers were also determined to create a sufficient sense of community, a sufficient sense of being American, that this country could survive. There is even a negative side to this communal thrust in American history: at times the pressure toward conformity in American life is painfully high. It is almost as though we all realize that we can philosophically tolerate creeds of extreme liberalism because we know of the bracing pressures for conformity in this society. In effect, the founding fathers had two objectives: to control tyranny but to avoid the individualism and separation that could breed anarchy. Is it possible that to secure the first a nation needs a strong sense of negative liberty, whereas to secure the second it needs a strong sense of positive liberty? In any event, there is a communal side to the American political tradition as well as an individual side even though the latter has received far more attention because it is a unique American contribution.

Finally, the Reagan administration's approach is wrong because it fails that most important of American political tests: it is not very pragmatic and in any struggle that, as Einstein suggested, can never end, there must be a marriage between pragmatism and principle if constant defeat is to be avoided. The United States cannot expect other nations to pay special heed to its ideas if it refuses to listen to the ideas of others. As we have seen, the philosophical and practical distinctions between positive and negative freedom may not be as sharp as Berlin suggested if one assumes that citizens in most countries of ethnic and religious diversity are not as law-abiding as Oxford dons.

The Dilemmas of Implementation

Nonetheless, we are left with a dilemma. Even if we know the human rights we want to promote, that is, even if we accept that we should be promoting both negative and positive rights, we are not terribly sure we know how to go about it. Elliott Abrams, the Assistant Secretary of State for Human Rights, in a September 1982 address to the Chicago World

Affairs Council, has called attention to the difference between the Morality of Intentions and the Morality of Results.[8]

The curse of any human rights policy, he points out, is that we may intend one result and end up with another. Many of the debates over the Carter human rights policies concern allegations about this distinction. Right-wing critics charge that the Carter administration followed a morality of intentions and ended up with an immorality of results. It wanted democracy and decency in Iran and ended up with the Ayatollah's cruel dictatorship. It intended to favor the overthrow of the cruel but friendly dictatorship in Nicaragua in the hope of gaining a decent and friendly democracy in that country and ended up with the cruel and unfriendly dictatorship of the Sandinistas.

Left-wing critics, in contrast, charge the Carter administration not with an excess of good intentions but with an absence of good intentions. They note that far from being a consistent critic of human rights abuses wherever they might occur, President Carter embraced the regime of the Shah of Iran during the presidential visit to Teheran, sent a letter to Somoza commending him for his human rights progress, was silent on human rights abuses in China because a louder voice might have interfered with the normalization process between the two countries, and generally allowed national security considerations to silence American human rights policies toward such militarily significant allies as the Philippines and South Korea.

Two such sharply contrasting views of the same events suggest that those who conduct our foreign policy face some excruciating difficulties. For Secretary Abrams is correct: the gap between the morality of intentions and the morality of results does exist, and the reason is that human events are influenced by human emotions and do not therefore follow any readily predictable course. On this point Machiavelli once illuminated the dilemma statesmen face when he wrote: "Fortune is arbiter of half of our actions but she leaves the control of the other half to us."[9] What that means is that we regard our political leaders as sufficiently in control for us to hold them responsible for their actions; but they may not be sufficiently in control for us to judge fairly just how responsible for their actions they really are. This random character of public life explains both its cruelty and its high rewards. Men rise because they are credited with successes they did little to promote. They fall when they are charged with failure they tried valiantly to avoid.

Machiavelli's percentages, however, are even less reassuring than these observations may suggest. For there is a fundamental difference between the pursuit of policy goals at the domestic level and their pursuit at the international level. At the domestic level a body of law and a structure of institutions exist to rein in passions and manage the struggle for power. At the domestic level on some issues a statesman's control over fortune may be considerably more than 50 per cent. But at the international level, where law exists but is not respected and the United Nations structure survives but is seldom used, our control over fortune may be considerably less. And the fear lurking in everyone's mind is that in the pursuit of freedom we may achieve anarchy.

Two historical examples may shed some light on this problem. Historians have documented the extent to which the Czech government was mistreating the Sudeten German population prior to Hitler's demand that these German-speaking areas be incorporated into his Third German Reich. And there can be little doubt that the populations in question preferred the dictatorial rule of Hitler to the democratic rule of the Czechs and Slovaks. But in their decision to honor the right to self determination of the Sudeten Germans, Britain and France also knuckled under to German threats and pressure, deprived Czechoslovakia of a strategic region it absolutely required if it were to defend itself against Nazi arms, and in many ways, directly and indirectly, helped create the climate of anarchy, opportunity, and aggression that led to World War II.

In the last century a similar kind of problem faced the international community. Ever since the end of the Napoleonic wars the question of whether Russia should take over the heritage of the Turkish Empire and its frontiers to the Mediterranean had threatened Europe with war. This so-called Eastern Question led to the Crimean War in 1854–56. Twenty years later some of the Balkan people revolted against the Turkish sultan, who put the rebellion down with terrible brutality. In England the great liberal politician, William E. Gladstone, denounced the "Bulgarian horrors" and urged international action. But in reply one leading British journal contended that it was quite proper that 12 or 13 million Christians in Turkey should remain unhappy rather than that 200 million men in India should be deprived of the benefits of British rule and then 30 million Englishmen made uncomfortable by the apprehension of such a catastrophe.[10] (A more modern statement of the position comes from France. When France signed a gas pipeline contract with the Soviet Union December 1981, French Prime Minister Pierre Mauroy explained: "One must not add to the Polish drama the suffering of gas consumers in France.")

Of course, the key word in the statement of the British journal is "unhappy." The Christians in Bulgaria were more than unhappy. Many of them were dead because of the severe Turkish repression. Nevertheless, beneath its flippancy, the magazine's comment suggests a problem with morality in international affairs that continues to trouble us to this day. About the time that Gladstone was denouncing the "Bulgarian horrors," his great conservative rival Benjamin Disraeli was writing a friend privately that he refused to "avenge Bulgarian atrocities by the butchery of the world."[11]

What should be the attitude of the international community toward the fate of people when a change in their national status threatens international stability? An initial approach is to recognize the force of the phenomenon with which we are dealing. Once again, I turn to Berlin for a classic formulation of this issue.

Berlin traces the demand for self-determination to the need in every human being for recognition of his own worth and existence. He writes:

> For if I am not so recognized, then I may fail to recognize, I may doubt, my own claim to be a fully independent human being. For what I am is, in large part, determined by what I feel and think; and what I feel and think is determined by the feeling and thought prevailing in the society to which I belong, of which, in Burke's sense, I form not an isolable atom, but an ingredient . . . in a social pattern. I may feel unfree in the sense of not being recognized as a self-governing individual human being; but I may feel it also as a member of an unrecognized or insufficiently respected group: then I wish for the emancipation of my entire class, or community, or nation, or race, or profession. So much can I desire this, that I may, in my bitter longing for status, prefer to be bullied and misgoverned by some member of my own race or social class, by whom I am, nevertheless, recognized as a man and a rival—that is as an equal—to being well and tolerantly treated by someone from some higher and remoter group.[12]

No one can listen to these words and not recognize their strength. They explain not only the relentless Palestinian desire for a homeland but on the domestic scene they also explain black power and ethnic politics in city after city in this land.

The claims of each of these groups for recognition are valid, but they have an unfortunate side effect. They arouse fears and animosity among other groups. On the one hand, if valid claims for recognition are ignored, pressures build with no outlet until suddenly there is a violent eruption whose extreme dimensions few can predict beforehand. On the other hand, to vent the pressure prematurely, without adequate concern for the rights and security of others, also courts disaster.

As difficult as it is to deal with such problems domestically, it is infinitely more difficult internationally. For, as we have noted, the international community does not benefit from a clear framework of respected laws. Nor is there any centralization of force in the international community to isolate and limit an individual state's resort to force. An action taken for human rights considerations does not cause other states to comply but rather permits them to reassess their interests and opportunities for new gains internationally. The conclusions they reach may validate Disraeli's fear about an international response to the "Bulgarian horrors"; the world may be plunged into "butchery" of even larger dimensions. The new realism in human rights therefore calls for caution as a discipline to concern; and it calls for prudence as a brake on posturing. The call is neither for prolonged inaction that increases the pressure nor for premature initiatives that also increase it from new directions.

The Terrible Sublime

Our own history should be instructive in this regard. For the United States attempted to cap a veritable political volcano through a constitutional provision permitting slavery to continue, even though thoughtful statesmen at the time understood the danger the Republic was running. John

Quincy Adams, once asked for his evaluation of Jefferson, wrote these prescient words:

> Jefferson is one of the great men this country has produced, one of the men who has contributed largely to the formation of our national character—to much that is good and to not a little that is evil in our sentiments and manners. His Declaration of Independence is an abridged Alcaron of political doctrine, laying open the first foundations of civil society; but he does not appear to have been aware that it also laid open a precipice into which the slaveholding planters of his country sooner or later must fall. With the Declaration of Independence on their lips, and the merciless scourge of slavery in their hands, a more flagrant image of human inconsistency can scarcely be conceived than one of our Southern slaveholding republicans. Jefferson has been himself all his life a slaveholder, but he has published opinions so blasting to the very existence of slavery, that, however credible they may be to his candor and humanity, they speak not much for his prudence or his forecast as a Virginian planter. The seeds of the Declaration of Independence are yet maturing. The harvest will be what West, the painter, calls the terrible sublime.[13]

America struggled for decades to avoid the "terrible sublime" because addressing the issue prematurely would have destroyed the country. When we finally did address the issue, the country almost was destroyed. Against this history, we should have far more sympathy with the efforts of other countries to avoid the "terrible sublime" than we often do.

Some human rights scholars have noted that the United States interest in human rights was most intense at two very different periods in our history: at the time of the American Revolution and today. We appreciate the concern at the time of the American Revolution, but why the concern today?

The most direct answer is that decades too late the United

States finally faced up to the social cancer within its own breast—the plight of minorities within the United States itself. So long as the United States ignored this problem, it confronted the world Janus-faced: one side the face of hope; the other side the face of shame. It was the American recognition that its own record was terribly marred that prevented this country until recently from being the kind of consistent advocate of human rights that one might expect, given the political traditions and popular attitudes of the country.

But more is at work than renewed United States concern. It has been widely noted that the United States Executive Branch did not initiate the human rights movement. Indeed, the people were the real initiators. And the people in question were not only Americans. This has rightly been called an age of political participation, but it might equally well be described as an age of political resistance. For all over the world—to different degrees to be sure—the trend is not only to demand efficiency from governments in the management of programs that benefit people, but also restraint in the actions that harm them. All over the world people are resisting authority more than they used to. And their resistance is engendering a widening circle of support.

During the Helsinki negotiations it was West European governments, not the United States government, that insisted on inclusion of the human rights items. The European governments were, however, not acting solely out of some high-minded concern with the obligations of United Nations member states under the Universal Declaration of Human Rights. They were responding to vigorous demands from their electorates for progress in the field of human rights. Europeans ask with increasing insistence for an end to the artificial division of their continent. They demand that progress begin at the human level so that families can be reunited and Europeans can begin to address one another again as inhabitants of a region that enjoys common ties, a common history, and a common future.

Nor is the human rights movement limited to Western countries. There are important stirrings in every continent and in every political system. In China, Democracy Wall appeared with eloquent pleas for greater respect for human rights; in the Soviet Union there has been a cautious debate in the Soviet press among lawyers concerning the assumptions of innocence or guilt of an accused and the pressure that is apparently now applied to courts and the KGB to follow proper legal procedures; in June 1981, the Organization of African Unity Assembly of Heads of State and Government approved an African Charter of Human and People's Rights. The Charter will come into force upon ratification by a simple majority of the member states. By the end of 1982, sixteen states had signed the Charter, and six of those had formally deposited the instruments of ratification.

Within the United Nations slow but encouraging progress has been registered. The 38th (1982) session of the United Nations Human Rights Commission adopted a resolution expressing its deep concern over the widespread violations of human rights and fundamental freedoms in Poland. For the first time in its 38-year history the Commission spoke out on human rights violations in an East European country, even though the report that resulted from that decision leaves much to be desired. Earlier, during the Carter administration, the Commission for the first time took up new human rights cases in Latin America and Africa and no longer restricted itself to routine denunciations of Chile, Israel, and South Africa.

Why is all this happening? Some Americans believe that it is American interest or leadership alone that has caused this change. And certainly it would be hard to deny that the fact that the United States has taken an interest plays a role. But something much more fundamental than United States pressure or concern is involved. Arthur Schlesinger, Jr., has called attention to the contribution that Alexis de Tocqueville had made to our understanding of the development of what we might call humanitarianism in the last few centuries:

> Tocqueville persuasively attributed the humanitarian ethic to the rise of the idea of equality. In aristocratic societies, he wrote, those in the upper caste hardly believe that their inferiors "belong to the same race." When medieval chroniclers "relate the tragic end of a noble, their grief flows apace; whereas they tell you at a breath and without wincing of massacres and tortures inflicted on the common sort of people." Tocqueville recalled the "cruel jocularity" with which the intelligent and delightful Madame de Sévigné, one of the most civilized women of the seventeenth century, described the breaking on a wheel of an itinerant fiddler "for getting up a dance and stealing some stamped paper." It would be wrong, Tocqueville observed, to suppose that Madame de Sévigné was selfish or sadistic. Rather, she "had no clear notion of suffering in anyone who was not a person of quality."[14]

Lest we think that this callous attitude toward others is characteristic of another age, we need only recall that the worst human rights abuses of this century have also been possible because one group did not regard another as its equal. The concept of a master race or a social class more progressive than all others is vital to the development of the worst forms of repression. Where such concepts can lead is seen in the words of the Bolshevik leader Nikolai Bukharin, ironically one of the more liberal Bolsheviks, when he wrote in 1920: "Proletarian coercion, in all its forms, from executions to forced labour, is, paradoxical as it may sound, the method of moulding communist humanity out of the human material of the capitalist period."[15] The proletariat through its dictatorship, like the fascists through their conquests, in other words, arrogate to themselves the right to "mould humanity" to create an allegedly better world.

But we do not have to look for brutality on the scale of the communist purges or Hitler's concentration camps to see the degree to which Tocqueville has provided an insight both into the cause of the more serious human rights abuses in the world and into the rising concern throughout the world for a greater respect for human rights. For how does the ranch hand in Colombia differ from Madame de Sévigné when, as news accounts tell us still happens, he may hunt down primitive Indians in the Colombian jungles for sport the way he would hunt down a wild animal? Do we not all understand psychological implications of designating all Vietnamese as "gooks" when we probe the tragedy at My Lai? What attitudes toward the Palestinians as a people did some senior Israeli army officers harbor that permitted them to be indifferent to the fate of the women and children in the camps of Sabra and Shatila? Did the Christian perpetrators of the massacres in those camps think they were working for a higher order in Lebanon when they commenced the killing? It is known that the Christian officer who ordered the soldiers not to ask again what they should do with the Palestinian women and children laughed after he issued his order. Was his soldier's laugh any different from the "cruel jocularity" attributed to Madame de Sévigné?

These events demonstrate that it remains relatively easy for individuals and groups, even today, to dehumanize others to the point that their oppression or worse does not seem to be a crime. Yet it also seems true that it is becoming more difficult to practice the more extreme forms of dehumanization. The concept of spaceship earth, a vessel in which all are fellow passengers, may not have gained enough strength to weaken seriously the prerogatives of the sovereign nation-state, but the concept has acquired enough credence to give a major boost to human rights worldwide. Thus, Americans may fear the Soviet government, but they do not hate Russians the way they once thought they hated the Germans or the Japanese. Russians fear American strength and intentions, but any American visitor to the Soviet Union can confirm for you that Russians do not hate Americans.

Communications have made all states more permeable than they once were. The cassette recorder, the Xerox machine, and the direct-dial telephone have revolutionized diplomacy. Citizens of different countries know more about one another than they ever did before. During the Polish crisis, whenever an American scholar doubted press reports of Solidarity's actions, those who spoke Polish had only to pick up the phone and dial directly the various personalities of the Polish labor movement. Until recently, American Jews have been able to dial directly their relatives in the Soviet Union to confirm or deny that they were having trouble with the emigration authorities. Nothing was more destructive to the Shah's rule than the arrival of the cassette recorder, which allowed the Ayatollah to disseminate his message throughout Iran. Probably the factor that does most to explain the continuation of the resistance to the Soviet invasion of Afghanistan is the power of modern communications. For through this technology the various resistance movements in Afghanistan realize that they are not alone. They do not lose hope because they understand that there is an overwhelming majority in the country that agrees with them, that there are others who are also paying the supreme sacrifice to force the Soviets to leave their country.

There is also another impact of communications. It is fashionable among more cultivated circles to stress the degree to which people are different from one another. The more we learn about others, so it is said, the more we realize that we were right to dislike them in the first place. But that is not the way that the ordinary person views it. Modern communications have enabled more and more people in every country to realize that all men and women belong to the same class of humanity. As a result, while wars may still take place and men and women may die in the service of their country, it is harder to work up the degree of fanaticism that makes gross violations of human rights as widely acceptable as they once were. The Archbishop of Canterbury was speaking for many when, though he angered the British government for his sentiments, he stressed the common humanity between Argentina and the United Kingdom in the aftermath of the recent Falklands war. The peace movement in Israel was speaking from a similar point of view. We must all do what we can to strengthen that sense of common humanity.

The Future Agenda

How do we foster that sense of humanity? There are several ways.

First, there has to be a general understanding that America cannot impose its values on the rest of the world. It can so practice those values in its national life that others will follow out of respect and admiration. John Quincy Adams remains correct when he suggests that the best way for America to encourage human rights is by "the countenance of her voice, and the benignant sympathy of her example."

Samuel Huntington, professor of government at Harvard University, pushes this argument in a new direction. In his words: "The power of example works only when it is an example of power. If the United States plays a strong, confident, preeminent role on the world stage, other nations will be impressed by its power and will attempt to emulate its liberty in the belief that liberty may be the source of power."[16]

No one can deny that weak states emulate the strong. When fascism was strong and apparently successful in a major country like Germany, fascist movements sprang up in countries throughout the world. When Nazi Germany fell, those movements receded even without a push from the victorious allies.

Nor can there be much doubt that after World War II many developing countries raced to set up Westminster forms of government not only because Britain wanted it that way but also because "democracy" had won the war. It had proved the superiority of its social and political system by prevailing. We should not derive too much comfort from the West's victory, however. The Soviet Union also won the war and by at least that standard might claim vindication of its social and political system.

The weakness of the Huntington approach is that liberties adopted for the reason he suggests will always be shallowly rooted. The first time the United States suffers a serious international setback, human rights also will suffer. Is this what has been happening? Quite the contrary has taken place. There has been an ebbing in United States influence, which has declined as United States domination of the world economy has receded and as a result of America's disastrous defeat in Vietnam. According to the Huntington thesis, these setbacks should have marked a period when liberties themselves receded. But the opposite happened. The first seedlings of liberty began to develop in the communist world. The human rights revolution began in the 1970s when foreign perceptions of American power were less flattering than they had been at any point in the postwar period.

Huntington is certainly right that were the United States ever to fall, the democratic ideal would suffer a devastating reversal throughout the world. There would be an echo effect in other societies. In that sense American power is vital to the survival of the democratic ideal. But mere power is not enough. How it is exercised is equally important, particularly in an international environment where America is not omnipotent and must persuade in order to prevail.

Second, the United States can recognize that political and economic rights are interconnected. It can accord the same sympathy to other states struggling to realize those rights that much of the rest of the world accorded the United States for 100 years as it attempted to confront the central contradiction of its national life—its ideal of human equality and its reality of racial inequality. Such an approach would not mean that the United States would excuse others' failure to follow the provisions of the Universal Declaration of Human Rights, but it would require the United States to acknowledge "best efforts" where they occur, and this acknowledgment should take into account the very different political and economic conditions governments face. A state that is trying to contain an incipient civil war cannot follow the same high standard as a politically homogeneous state enjoying international security and domestic peace. A nation struggling with massive poverty and backwardness will have different priorities from a state blessed with affluence.

Third, the United States must work to ensure that information on human rights is open, objective, and consistent. Thus it probably is a mistake for the United States to entrust to the State Department the preparation of the annual survey of human rights in the world; for the State Department's role is to enhance the influence and protect the interests of the United States in the world. At times, at least in the short run, this role may conflict with its current responsibility for monitoring human rights in the world. That responsibility might logically be given to the Library of Congress, to which the State Department would be required to submit information that the Library would combine with information from other sources.

Fourth, the United States must recognize that human rights in other countries as in the United States are best protected not by international concern, as useful as that on occasion may be, but by local institutions. The blacks in the United States were little helped by international condemnations of the conditions in which they lived; they were greatly helped by the existence of institutions in the United States, primarily the courts, that began to protect their rights. The foremost objective of the United States should therefore be the development or the encouragement of local and regional institutions in other countries that can be the principal guardians of human rights at the local level. India and Mexico, among others, have advanced initiatives in this direction. They should be encouraged through American rhetoric and financial support.

Fifth, the United States must make sacrifices for human rights but at the prudent margin. It would be a mistake to reorient the United States aid program strictly to accord with human rights criteria but current policies are even more mistaken. A short-run use of the American aid program almost exclusively to support United States security objectives could bring gratitude today and instability tomorrow.

For geopolitical reasons the United States cannot establish a relationship with India as close as their respective democratic forms of government might imply, but the United States should work harder than it has to praise and reward large Third World states like India or Venezuela that are attempting to develop democratic societies. Within the communist world the United States must proceed with determination but prudence. Only the people of those countries can democratize themselves. A crusade for democracy will be an utter failure if it is harnessed to the American geopolitical chariot. But it can succeed over time if it reflects the good will and continuing interest of American society. The administration should radically adjust its current plans and turn the proposed budget of the crusade for democracy entirely over to nonprofit organizations that represent the democratic ideal in our country. The American government itself can have the courage to acknowledge that while the degree of the violation of human rights in Eastern Europe remains egregious, some progress has been made. Eastern Europe is a more decent place to live than it was twenty years ago. We have only to recall that after the Hungarian revolution those defeated were swinging from the gallows. In Poland the goverment is reluctant to bring many members of Solidarity to trial; no one has been executed. In short, our condemnations must be courageous but so also must our balance.

Finally, we must recognize that time is on the side of the crusade for human rights. Orwell's predictions about what governments would attempt to do have been proven correct. Many modern governments have resorted to the Big Lie in asserting that freedom is slavery or that true liberty is attained through absolute obedience to the party or the nation. But Orwell's predictions about human nature have been proven wrong. Despite decades of the Big Lie, individuals throughout the world recognize the very differences that authoritarian governments have struggled to blur. These men and women await only their moment to claim the freedoms that their governments contend on paper they have never been denied.

Notes

1. Albert Einstein, Address to the Chicago Decalogue Society, February 20, 1954.
2. Isaiah Berlin, *Four Essays on Liberty* (Oxford: Oxford University Press, 1969), 121.
3. Ibid., 122.
4. Ibid., 125.

5. Ibid., 124.

6. *Country Reports on Human Rights Practices for 1982*, United States Department of State Report Submitted to the Committee on Foreign Affairs of the U.S. House of Representatives and the Committee on Foreign Relations of the U.S. Senate, Joint Committee Print, Washington, D.C.

7. Berlin, 129.

8. Elliott Abrams, Speech before the Chicago World Affairs Council, September 29, 1982.

9. Niccolo Machiavelli, *The Prince*, XXV.

10. Hans J. Morgenthau and Kenneth W. Thompson, *Principles & Problems of International Politics* (New York: Knopf, 1950), 53–54.

11. Ibid., 54.

12. Berlin, 157.

13. Paul A. Varg, *Foreign Policies of the Founding Fathers* (East Lansing, Michigan: Michigan State University Press, 1963), 147–148.

14. Alexis de Tocqueville, *Democracy in America, Volume II*, Book 3, Chapter 1, (New York: The Colonial Press, 1975).

15. Berlin, 137.

16. Samuel Huntington, "American Ideals versus American Institutions," *Political Science Quarterly*, 97 (Spring 1982), 33.

Appendix: The Virginia Declaration of Rights

[12 June 1776]

A Declaration of Rights made by the Representatives of the good people of Virginia, assembled in full and free Convention; which rights do pertain to them and their posterity, as the basis and foundation of Government.

1. That all men are by nature equally free and independent, and have certain inherent rights, of which, when they enter into a state of society, they cannot, by any compact, deprive or divest their posterity; namely, the enjoyment of life and liberty, with the means of acquiring and possessing property, and pursuing and obtaining happiness and safety.

2. That all power is vested in, and consequently derived from, the People; that magistrates are their trustees and servants, and at all times amenable to them.

3. That Government is, or ought to be, instituted for the common benefit, protection, and security of the people, nation, or community;—of all the various modes and forms of Government that is best which is capable of producing the greatest degree of happiness and safety, and is most effectually secured against the danger of mal-administration;—and that, whenever any Government shall be found inadequate or contrary to these purposes, a majority of the community hath

an indubitable, unalienable, and indefeasible right, to reform, alter, or abolish it, in such manner as shall be judged most conducive to the publick weal.

4. That no man, or set of men, are entitled to exclusive or separate emoluments and privileges from the community, but in consideration of publick services; which, not being descendible, neither ought the offices of Magistrate, Legislator, or Judge, to be hereditary.

5. That the Legislative and Executive powers of the State should be separate and distinct from the Judicative; and, that the members of the two first may be restrained from oppression, by feeling and participating the burdens of the people, they should, at fixed periods, be reduced to a private station, return into that body from which they were originally taken, and the vacancies be supplied by frequent, certain, and regular elections, in which all, or any part of the former members, to be again eligible, or ineligible, as the law shall direct.

6. That elections of members to serve as Representatives of the people, in Assembly, ought to be free; and that all men, having sufficient evidence of permanent common interest with, and attachment to, the community, have the right of suffrage, and cannot be taxed or deprived of their property for publick uses without their own consent or that of their Representative so elected, nor bound by any law to which they have not, in like manner, assented, for the publick good.

7. That all power of suspending laws, or the execution of laws, by any authority, without consent of the Representatives of the people, is injurious to their rights, and ought not to be exercised.

8. That in all capital or criminal prosecutions a man hath a right to demand the cause and nature of his accusation, to be confronted with the accusers and witnesses, to call for evidence in his favour, and to a speedy trial by an impartial jury

of his vicinage, without whose unanimous consent he cannot be found guilty, nor can he be compelled to give evidence against himself; that no man be deprived of his liberty except by the law of the land, or the judgment of his peers.

9. That excessive bail ought not to be required, nor excessive fines imposed, nor cruel and unusual punishments inflicted.

10. That general warrants, whereby any officer or messenger may be commanded to search suspected places without evidence of a fact committed, or to seize any person or persons not named, or whose offence is not particularly described and supported by evidence, are grievous and oppressive, and ought not to be granted.

11. That in controversies respecting property, and in suits between man and man, the ancient trial by Jury is preferable to any other, and ought to be held sacred.

12. That the freedom of the Press is one of the greatest bulwarks of liberty, and can never be restrained but by despotick Governments.

13. That a well-regulated Militia, composed of the body of the people, trained to arms, is the proper, natural, and safe defence of a free State; that Standing Armies, in time of peace, should be avoided as dangerous to liberty; and that, in all cases, the military should be under strict subordination to, and governed by, the civil power.

14. That the people have a right to uniform Government; and, therefore, that no Government separate from, or independent of, the Government of Virginia, ought to be erected or established within the limits thereof.

15. That no free Government, or the blessing of liberty, can be preserved to any people but by a firm adherence to justice, moderation, temperance, frugality, and virtue, and by frequent recurrence to fundamental principles.

16. That Religion, or the duty which we owe to our

Creator, and the manner of discharging it, can be directed only by reason and conviction, not by force or violence; and, therefore, all men are equally entitled to the free exercise of religion, according to the dictates of conscience; and that it is the mutual duty of all to practise Christian forbearance, love, and charity, towards each other.

Index